POTTY
MOUTH

POTTY MOUTH

A woman disabled with multiple sclerosis bravely meets life's challenges with courage, wisdom, and a profane sense of humor.

By Renae Clare

authorHOUSE®

AuthorHouse™
1663 Liberty Drive
Bloomington, IN 47403
www.authorhouse.com
Phone: 1-800-839-8640

Published by AuthorHouse   05/03/2012

ISBN: 978-1-4685-6240-8 (sc)
ISBN: 978-1-4685-6239-2 (e)

Library of Congress Control Number: 2012904461

Any people depicted in stock imagery provided by Thinkstock are models,
and such images are being used for illustrative purposes only.
Certain stock imagery © Thinkstock.

This book is printed on acid-free paper.

Because of the dynamic nature of the Internet, any web addresses or links
contained in this book may have changed since publication and may no longer be
valid. The views expressed in this work are solely those of the author and do not
necessarily reflect the views of the publisher, and the publisher hereby disclaims
any responsibility for them.

This book is dedicated to my children, Ryan and Lara. They have both grown up to be wonderful people and my wish is to make them proud.

CONTENTS

FOREWORD

Have you ever met another person and suddenly, inexplicably felt as though you were standing under a beam of sunlight? That's what it is like to meet Renae. Even though she came to me to heal, even while depressed, the warmth of her personality broke through clearly. There was a resilience there that was almost palpable, a strength that was, although clear to me, still amorphous and fleeting to her.

Renae often thanks me for what I have done for her; she has little conception of what she has done for me. Since I specialize in treating patients with physical health problems, particularly multiple sclerosis, I have the opportunity to witness a myriad of coping strategies when one deals with a disabling disease. Rarely do I have the good fortune of meeting an individual like Renae, someone who has fully accepted her compromised physical condition, who has accepted life in a wheelchair.

She did not come to me because she was grieving the loss of her legs; she came to me because she was haunted by old ghosts, and now that she was restricted to her chair, she had the time and inclination to conquer and develop the other parts of her that had remained dormant or unhealed. Renae understood that she was more than her body, bigger than her body; she already understood when she came to me she also had an emotional body, a spiritual body, a mental body—all of which were intact but some of which were bleeding. She also understood that her physical body put strain on some of the people who were close to her, so she set forth on a determined path to become as independent as she possibly could, in every way that she could.

The first time I saw her, her daughter brought her to therapy; it was clear to me that although Renae was very motivated to attend sessions once a week, she was reluctant to put her young, busy, working daughter out week after week. One mention of contacting another alternative (the Handi-ride bus, a Dallas-based transportation system developed for disabled people) was all it took—during our next session, she told me that she had signed up and was awaiting approval. This is a good example of what it is like to have Renae as a patient—every therapist's dream, because she actually used the information discussed in the session. Despite feeling helpless at the time, she believed she had choices and was eager to exercise those choices. There is no sign of self-pity or self-destructiveness in this woman; she was like a thirsty plant that, with just a bit of water, began to regrow her stems.

If a patient has enough courage to stay with the therapy process, as it progresses, it can become, for a time, much more difficult than perhaps expected. Patients often begin canceling appointments right around this time, afraid to delve more deeply into the murky depths of their psyches, afraid of what they will find, afraid of what cannot be healed. Afraid of what can. During this time with Renae, she continued to come, on time, on her bus, alone—100 degree weather, 20 degree weather, she was always there, a blanket on her legs in the wintertime, a bottle of water in the summer. With her telltale honesty, she would always tell me how she felt ("Damn it, I really didn't want to come to see you today! Fucking Dr. Cinzia!"), but she showed up. This is how Renae approaches her whole life—she might not have liked losing her ability to walk, and she hated being abused by a bevy of men, but she continued to show up in her life, present and willing to heal and move on.

This book is not just about a woman who has a disability or the experience of having a disability; it is not about how men can be "Fuckwads." It is about one woman's journey toward self-healing; it is about courage and strength; and it is about how, in the face of anything, the human spirit is capable of persevering.

Dr. Cinzia Levalds

Following "Stuck", is the first writing that I showed to Dr. Cinzia when we first met when she asked me why I was there and why I needed help. I had lost my sense of self, my spiritual self, and the real me, who was hidden by so much baggage and so much of the past that I had been dragging around with me for the past fifty-seven years of my unsure and guilt ridden life. It was exhausting and sapping my creativity, my liveliness, my joyfulness, my independence, and my reason for living. And I longed to get all of that back.

Stuck

I'm stuck in this chair with wheels
and legs that don't work,
and I'm stuck in this body that won't move
when I tell it to, yell it to, scream it to, cry and
weep and sob it to.
Circuitry gone awry;

No way out, no way in, no way around
or between or through.
What to do; succumb, retreat, relent,
seep inside the self, the mind, the soul,
try to find peace, acceptance, dignity, joy, religion,
a reason to live; some love, some hope, some courage,
some faith, some miracle, some thing
that will relieve the ache of being forevermore
stuck.

1

ODE TO A GODDAMN SON OF A BITCH FUCKWAD
(NOT HIS REAL NAME)

Goddamn you! How could you treat me like that; say those horrible things to me; speak to me as though I were nothing, less than nothing; stun me so cruelly that I peed in my pants, cowered, and shrank almost to invisibility? And you did it over and over, every single day until I believed what you said. I felt stupid and worthless, and so now I know why abused women stay with their abuser. Because I was the abused and you were the abuser. Statistics say that it takes ten times as long to heal from psychological and verbal abuse than from physical abuse, if ever. It changes us. And it is the mental abuse, the psychological that I am working so hard to heal from, to forget, to forgive, and then to move on.

Where did that come from? When did that start? Was it when I had an abortion because I knew that my Multiple Sclerosis was getting worse and I wouldn't be able to do it? I would not be able to take care of the baby. I would not be able to be a good mother, and it would not be fair to this new child because with every pregnancy Multiple Sclerosis

1

symptoms magnify and I was already getting weaker? Is that why I went to the abortionist without you—because you said you needed to stay at the store and take care of business, and I had to ask Lara and Tommy to take me and wait for me so that I had a way to get back home? How humiliated I was to have to ask my daughter and her boyfriend to be my support during such a horrific experience. And never once did you ask me about that wicked deed or show any concern or ask if I was okay . . . Because I wasn't. I was relieved and heartsick at the same time. I thought about it for years afterward. It finally faded into the background, and life went on as usual.

I know your father physically and verbally abused your mom and you, and so intellectually, I understand the workings of that vicious cycle. It is the foulness and vehemence of your language that so rarely reared its ugly head toward me, and I thought that kind of abuse only happened to other women. It certainly wouldn't come into the home of two people who loved each other so much. So that when it did hit, I felt as though I'd been run over by a wheat harvester, by a cement mixer, by a manure spreader; seemingly out of nowhere, because at first I didn't know of your affair.

And even after I did find out, it was so shocking that you reverted back to behaviors that you remembered from your father. I imagine that it never even came to your consciousness that you were acting like him, only because you were doing it to me and I think it was to alienate me so extremely that I would have to be the one to end our marriage; you could simply move on. But God, I hung on, having nowhere to go, no one to turn to, no way to find help, and no money to be on my own. Multiply all of that by one hundred and add in MS, so that it was only the love for my children that has kept me alive.

Or was it that I was getting sicker and weaker, and that my illness, Multiple Sclerosis just wasn't in your plans?

Remember when you told me I walked like an old lady and I embarrassed you? I told you I walked like a woman with MS. I had to hold on to the walls of buildings as I walked down the street to keep from falling to my knees. You said nothing more and walked away. I cried, yet again. I tried so hard to keep a cheerful face, a cheerful demeanor. To show sadness or fear or fatigue was not an option. You loved me when I was strong. You respected me when I was able to perform—a great mom, a great businesswoman, and an awesome partner by your side through it all, a great lover until I couldn't move as well or was just plain exhausted.

I became an embarrassment, a burden, a leech sucking up all of your resources. I dragged you down, and you disapproved of my every move. I needed to take cabs to get Ryan back and forth from school—a waste of money when I should've been able to walk him to and from. My cooking was boring. Didn't you realize how hard it was to make great dinners when you would leave just enough money for me to shop and I could barely walk? So I often ordered groceries over the phone but had to include a delivery tip, and I had to pay for taxi fares whenever I needed to go anywhere. I saved up every dime, so how was I supposed to make gourmet meals? And I was so tired that just to cook a simple meal was just too much.

I understood . . . your devious statements . . . once I found out your lover is a gourmet cook and that she worked for a major airline company so you could travel free on her gift passes, and she would feed you wonderful gourmet meals when you traveled to Dallas and told me you were on business trips to Minnesota. And of course, she could fuck you in ways that I no longer could because I was losing feeling in my legs and fatigued most of the time. How could I possibly compete with the excitement of a brand-new relationship? You *liar*. You *cheater*. You *pig!*

At Christmas time one year, you brought home a box of fantastic home-baked goodies that were to die for. When I asked you who gave them to us, you had to think for a little bit and you told me that a customer made them to celebrate the holidays. Then I asked you which one and you really had to think. I could kind of see the wheels turning when you told me the name of the customer. I recognized who she was, and I gushed about how wonderful and thoughtful it was for her to do that for us. I told you that I was going to have to thank her in person for the gift and that I wanted her recipes for a couple of the goodies. At that time, I was clueless as to your goings-on, and even though I detected some apprehension on your part, it didn't really register until later on—those gourmet delicacies that you brought home for your wife and your child were actually sent by your lover. I really don't think that it was her intention for you to share her goodies with your wife.

You compared everything that I did to everything that she did for you. I didn't even know that she existed, but you let me know that I was subpar, that I wasn't holding up my end of the deal, and that I was the cause of all of your discontent and disapproval.

You conveniently forgot, you erased it from your memory, how all of my hard work and my passion for our businesses and my deep love for you were why you were able to be who you are. It never once crossed your mind that you were not man enough to help your wife cope with an illness with kindness and caring and empathy, but instead you were mean and cruel and belittled me even in front of other people, making it seem as though it was my entire fault, the stress making the MS worse and worse.

One time I was coming back to the store from someplace or other and I was beat. I needed to sit down and was having a hard time walking and taking the three steps to the front door of the store. Two of our employees and you were there talking, and as I came closer, clearly struggling, you told me I was slumping over. Right there in front of anyone within earshot. You did not offer to help me; you did not offer me a hand or kind word of sympathy or caring. I had embarrassed you once again. You thoughtless, mean brute.

The two guys standing by you were helpless to do anything, so I just straightened myself up and said, still smiling, doing my best to retain my dignity, "Oh, I didn't even realize it." But I sure did realize it and I'm sure that anyone who saw that interaction saw that you were the one who should have been embarrassed by your treatment of your wife, me, who had nothing to be embarrassed of, because being disabled in any way or getting MS was not my choice. You, however, had a choice about how to treat the mother of your child. If I had been a customer with MS and you saw me struggling,

I know that you would have helped and shown concern and led me to a place to sit down so I could gather my strength. The man that I knew for the first sixteen years of our eighteen years together would have stopped and spoken to me for a while and offered help and empathy before he went back to his business.

You knew I was sick and told people that I wasn't strong enough to handle the truth—that you had fallen in love with someone else. It would have been so much easier to accept that news if it were revealed to me in a straightforward manner, perhaps with you sitting down with me, with compassion, leaving me with my dignity. Instead, the way you delivered this news showed me a part of yourself that I never knew was there—a part that very few people ever have or ever will see. You made a fool of me by bringing your lover into our store so that our employees, and possibly some of our customers, knew you were cheating on me and you weren't even trying to hide it. You flaunted her and told me not to come into the store, as I wasn't needed that day or for many, many more days to come.

One day out of the blue, you told me that you'd made an appointment with a therapist and that we were going to go together. I was taken aback, but I was happy nonetheless. I didn't know what it meant, but a tiny spark had been lit. I thought we were going to go there together so we could get through this nightmare. I barely remember getting there, but I do know that you did not help me in or out of the car, and you acted very cold. When we got to the therapist's office, I sat on one end of the couch and you sat on the other. The therapist was sitting opposite us in a chair behind her desk. She introduced herself to me. You had obviously met her before so it was no surprise to her that I hobbled into her office using a cane. The therapist said very little, and then you started to speak to me and told me that you wanted a divorce and that you didn't love me anymore; you gave me several reasons why, among them was that I wasn't even present anymore, you felt like you had to do everything yourself, and that I just wasn't attractive to you anymore.

Meanwhile I was sobbing, shaking uncontrollably, with my head in my hands. I asked you if you brought me there, to a therapist's office, to tell me you were divorcing me. I told you I thought we had gone there to get therapy so we could at least try to heal the wounds felt between us. How could you bring me to a therapist's office to tell me you were divorcing me? It just didn't register to me. I was blown away. I was devastated. It was such a slap in the face. You were so cold and mean about it, even in the therapist's office. Somehow you managed to turn it around and told me that I had to know what was going on and that I had to know that that's why we were there. What a coward you were, having the whole thing set up with a therapist of your choosing who, I'm sure, advised you exactly how to go about doing this so that, yet again, you would have your backup, and I would be sitting there defenseless, in shock, and alone.

The amazing thing is that during this whole interaction, the therapist just sat and watched, never interjecting, never saying a word; she just watched a world fall apart right in front of her eyes without doing a goddamn fucking thing. That's one hell of a therapist, I'll tell you. The only thing she said as I was hobbling out of the door was that if I needed any help coping, I should just call her. Fat chance in fucking hell, you bitch! Did she really think I would call her for help after she just sat there while I disintegrated without offering a single word of solace or of comfort? Well, I guess you got what you paid for—a therapist to be there for you when you dropped the bomb.

On the way out of the office, I was a complete mess, and you didn't offer any words or take any action to help me. You angrily stomped way ahead of me as I stumbled along to the car. You offered me no help getting in the car or closing the door. I was still sobbing hysterically. On the ride home, there was a stone-cold silence. Even there, you couldn't stand to be with me, to look at me, or even to speak to me. You really wished I would disappear. You wished I would just die.

Remember when I seduced you? I had you sit on a kitchen stool, and I gave you a blow job. When you came in my mouth, you said we could never do that again because you felt like you were cheating on *her*! I was your *wife*! And I still had your come in my mouth when you walked away. I spit it out in a dish cloth and stumbled to the bathroom to clean out my mouth. I should have spit it in your face, but again, I was too stunned to do anything. What I wanted from the seduction was to feel again; I wanted you to put your hands in my hair and on my face, to touch me and feel the fire and passion that we had shared for so long. I wanted anything from you except the torture that you dished out so freely and easily as though it were second nature to you to abuse your disabled wife. Fuck you! Fuck you! Fuck you!

You have never once said you are sorry or even hinted at any regret for the hurt, pain, depression, and thoughts of suicide you caused or even one of the many unkind words you said; you have never apologized to me for *anything!* You've just gone about your life so fucking relieved to have me gone. There was a time toward the end when I gave it up to a higher power and just relented and moved to Dallas because I was literally afraid for my life; your threats were becoming more and more taunting and frightening, and you even suggested that something really bad might happen to me.

I still dream of you. Can you believe that? They are nightmares where I am sinking in mud or drowning or lost and I can't find my way back home; you are there in those dreams and never help me even though you know I am in trouble. I wonder when it will stop and I will no longer have this darkness—this thick, greasy, dirty, putrid fog, engulfing my every pore.

How could I allow you to control me, to change me, to numb me, to erase all of the fun parts of me? Now I could be writing about you, a goddamn son of a bitch fuckwad, or I could be talking about this goddamn son of a bitch fuckwad disease, Multiple Sclerosis. You both bring feelings of fear, helplessness, sadness, and oppression; you both sap my strength, vitality, gumption, and creativity; and you both crush my ability to look forward. Well, fuck the two of ya!

Goddamn Son of a Bitch Fuckwad is much too long of a name to call you, so I will skip the goddamn, and I will skip the Son of a Bitch, and I will just call you from here on in Fuckwad, even though the aforementioned first and second names still apply.

2

MOTHERFUCKING MS

On January 20, 2011, I will have lived fifty-nine years, and I still have so much to think about and so much to do and so much to come to terms with. I don't feel like a woman almost sixty years of age. When I was a kid growing up, I thought sixty was old. My grandparents died in their sixties, and Mom was sixty-six when she passed on.

Going to therapy once a week with Dr. Cinzia has given me a taste of optimism and has lessened my fear of this dreadful disease, Multiple Sclerosis and my fear of losing even more of my powers and control. I had lost sight of my real self by claiming my disability as the totality of me, and as a result, I had become a victim. I had lost sight of the fact that my uncontrollable body is just the house that my spirit lives in and is a vessel for me to learn and grow. How far I have come in my journey and how very much further I have yet to go!

When I first came to Texas, I worked as a receptionist. I was always waiting for the other shoe to drop, for the day when I could no longer walk, because I knew my body was weakening, and the MS was getting worse. I tried to hide it, even from myself, but the stress of hiding it came at a terrible cost. I was exhausted all the time, not just from the MS itself, but from thinking constantly about how to do what I needed to do without anyone knowing how much weaker I was getting physically and how much more stressed I was getting mentally. I fell so many times and had to have coworkers and even strangers help me get back on my feet; they had to pick me up and help me steady myself with the cane I was using at the time. I got up with a smile, telling everybody I was okay and acting as though I was taking it all in stride.

Many of those times, I would go into the bathroom or into my car and cry from the humiliation of it and the fear of not knowing how much longer I could hold on. Seeing the looks of concern and pity in their eyes was awful, so I got up and moved on, trying to keep my fear and suffering inside. I stuffed it deeper and deeper, never admitting to anyone what I was really feeling or what was really going on. I could not admit my fear and loathed the thought of other people thinking that I was weak and pitiful and quite possibly drunk. I hated the word *disabled*. I wanted everyone to see me as courageous, as a woman who went on no matter what. But inside, I was drowning; I was devastated. I felt weak and tired from doing my damndest to hide what was really going on. I felt that I was making a fool out of myself over and over again.

I remember one time being in the owner's office with my supervisor; we were talking about something or other, and I peed in my pants as I was standing there right in front of them. I was humiliated and just wanted to die because I couldn't stop it. I had no control. I was just thankful I had on dark pants. I don't think they even noticed, but I'm sure

I left a wet spot on the carpet. The look on my face must have been a mixture of horror from the possibility that they would notice and disgust with myself for not being able to control my own body. I fumbled my words and probably sounded like a jerk. I slithered out of there as best I could with my cane, my legs shaking and my arms straining with the effort of holding myself up for so long, just hoping that I wouldn't fall right there in the owner's office. I felt so weak and so terribly ashamed. I went to the bathroom and got myself together before I went back to work at my desk, where I sat pretending that everything was just fine.

I've learned so many new ways to handle things along the way that if I'd known then what I know now, I would have saved myself untold horrors and many dreadful, fearful incidences—far too many to count.

At one point, I had an intestinal infection that went on for months. I thought it was MS related, but it just kept getting worse and worse. My good friend Brian finally convinced me to see a doctor. After several prescriptions for antibiotics, which caused unbearable nightmares that allowed me very little sleep, I finally got that behind me. However, more traumatizing humiliation that I find it hard to believe I got through followed. I had uncontrollable diarrhea at work. I often had to call for backup to take my place at the reception desk, but sometimes, my replacement would take too long and I would have to shove paper towels into my pants so I wouldn't shit on my office chair.

You just never know how MS will affect you from one moment to the next. One morning, as I was driving up to my work building, I became extremely dizzy and I hit the gas pedal instead of the brake and crashed into the metal rail in front of the plate-glass doors. If the steel railing had not been there, I would've gone through the plate-glass doors and right into the building. The rail was bent to hell. My car was a mess, the front bumper in pieces and broken headlight bits all over the place. I hobbled around and picked up as many pieces as I could hoping it wouldn't look as bad as it was. I put them in my backseat. I backed up, doing even more damage in the process, and then I tried to drive the car, but I did not get very far. Fortunately, Brian was working nearby, so I called him in a panic, and he came and got me. He helped me get a tow truck to get my car into a body shop. I had a rental for two weeks.

I also had to explain to everyone at work how it had happened. The front of the building was a mess. I still can't believe I did that. Everybody was great about it, but my confidence was shattered yet again.

Fucking MS.

3

WITCH'S TIT

Last night, I did something really bad, something cruel, something gruesome and frightening and sickening. I don't suppose that a postmenopausal defense will be enough to justify this because I should've known better. I should have seen in advance what the result would be, but I never would have expected my own reaction to my own dirty deed. Why didn't I listen to that little voice in my head that was saying, "Beware! Beware! All ye who enter here?"

Even if someone would have warned me in advance or would have counseled me and even if someone had tried to take away that cruel, cruel weapon forcefully, even then I don't think I would have listened. I would not have heeded the dire warnings and would have scratched and clawed to keep that heavy weighted weapon of convenience.

Understand, please, that I am now fifty-seven years old and am, as the old adage goes, no spring chicken. Gravity is a naturally occurring, scientifically proven force. It affects us one and all in ways seen and unseen, helping us and aiding us or defying and taunting us. My once lovely breasts bear the brunt and give a vivid and garish view of a witch's tit. My once shapely and strong legs and thighs are now swollen and achy, and where they were once taut and firm, they are now flabby and puckered—never again to be whistled at when passing a construction site or admired by a lover while standing in front of a full-length mirror. And my once shapely and contoured chin is now doubled and working toward a triple.

I must tell you though that none of that is nearly the worst; the worst cannot be covered up by long-sleeved shirts or lovely autumn colors or by a snuggly blanket covering my MS stricken knees and legs. No, the worst, the very, very worst is the one menopausal aftermath that is truly hateful, and it takes diligence and a steady hand to keep in check. Menopausal ladies, and postmenopausal ladies as well, you know what it is.

It is the ever-growing facial hair. It grows fast and dark and thick. I have several moles on my face, which again reminds me of first of the three little pigs saying to the big bad wolf who then huffed and puffed and blew his house down, "Not by the hair of my chinny, chin, chin" Clusters of white bristles are popping out of my cheek and chin, and one stray black horse's hair is just sticking out of my upper lip, just living a life of its own with no shame whatsoever. I could actually save them up and sell them to the Fuller Brush Company (And by the way, they make great brushes.) That's how many of them there are.

My once-a-month cleanup became once a week and now is at least a twice-a-week session of plucking and tweezing and waxing and hunting for those sly little fuckers that only show up in a certain light, playing hide-and-seek until you finally get one! Aha! Gotcha! You little weasel, you can run but you cannot hide. Sure, the plucking and the waxing hurts like hell, but it's oh so satisfying when they, the enemies, finally die.

So last night, the thing that I did that I should've known better and that I must warn you women of a certain age or perhaps nationality, such as Italian or German or Russian or Greek, about, the really shockingly bad, frightening thing I did was to look at my face in a 3X magnifying mirror. What the hell! What is *that*? I nearly scared myself to death; it really took me aback. That damn mirror made all those stray hairs look even larger and more monstrous and a thousand times more hideous.

It took me a moment or two to compose myself. I really couldn't believe it! My whole face was fuzzy, and the moley hairs looked like wires growing out of my face. I could've been one of Batman's adversaries, Wire Woman.

I couldn't stop staring at the horror of it all; it was like watching a four-car pileup with bloody body parts thrown into the ditch. How long had I been walking around in the world like this? Little kids clinging to their mommies' shirttails would be screaming, "Mommy, Mommy, look, it's a witch!" And the mothers would be gathering the little ones to their sides and trying to reassure them by saying, "It is only a menopausal woman and she won't hurt us. She is probably more afraid of us than we are of her. Come along now. Let's go get those water balloons and see if you can hit Daddy on the head with them from the upstairs bedroom when he comes home from work. Won't that be fun?" I can't even begin to think about what those fucking teenagers would be saying about me just loud enough for me to hear.

Anyway . . . Ladies . . . heed my warning. Do it if you must, but please, please, I beg of you: do your research, study what increased male hormones and decreased female hormones will do to your physical body. Don't go into this blindly, foolishly, and unthinkingly. If you do this with planning, forethought, and awareness, you will come out of it unscathed, and then you will know the face of your enemy and how best to exterminate it.

I too will recover from that dastardly deed. I did it in ignorance. I was a dumbass. Just remember, you are not alone, nor am I. I take solace in knowing that gravity is affecting everyone; even those fucking wise-ass teenagers who think nothing will ever happen to them. No fucking hairs on their fucking chinny fucking chins. I'll take solace in that thought and go forth boldly—sagging tits, hairy moles, flabby arms, cottage cheese ass, and all the rest of it, including the yeast infection in the creases of my inner thighs and the eczema on the middle finger of my right hand.

4

Secrets In The Nazi Closet

My uncle Tommy who was my Mom's younger brother died a few days ago when he fell down the stairs, supposedly drunk. I'm not sure about the drunken part but I certainly can believe it. He lived in Washington State and we were no longer close in distance or in spirit. Once upon a time, all six of the kids in my family adored Uncle Tommy who lived on a farm with Grandma and Grandpa about half an hour from ours. We spent every Sunday there and every holiday and we loved him so much. He was so much fun and he played with us and joked around with us and even Dad never had a harsh word to say about him which is extraordinary because Dad usually has a harsh word about everyone.

What little I know about his growing up is that it was pretty harsh. My great aunt and uncle also lived on that farm but in a separate house with their kids and I was told that Tommy and Kenneth, his cousin, got the tar beaten out of them many times and they took the brunt of the abuse. Those were the Depression years and life was very hard and sparse and they grew up in tough times in tough circumstances.

My family always seemed to have food on the table because we grew everything ourselves. Tommy and my grandparents raised pigs and chickens, ducks, and turkeys as well as a very big garden whereas our family raised beef and chickens and sometimes pigs as well as grain crops: wheat, barley and corn and of course we had a huge vegetable garden. We as children worked very hard helping with the animals and the garden, milking cows, helping with the butchering of steers and chickens for food. We learned how to do the canning and planting and harvesting and cooking and we all learned a great work ethic.

Mom and all of her kids, six in total, were in charge of butchering the chickens, up to 50 in one day. We would have to catch the chickens, get their heads on a post, and mom would chop their heads off and then let them go quickly because blood was spouting out of their necks. They were jumping around all over the place scaring that shit out of us. They actually seemed to be chasing us so we were all running around screaming trying to get away from the wild beasts. Sometimes the head was still attached by a little bit of skin and so the chicken would be jumping around already dead, with its head flopping wildly up-and-down. It literally is where the saying "running around like a chicken with its head cut off" came from.

When Dad first came home with the little chicks they came in boxes with separate compartments for each one to store them in and it would be with great pleasure and excitement that we would take the fluffy little yellow chicks out and put them on the ground in the chicken coop and snuggle and play with them. They were so cute and so soft and it was pure joy to see 100 little chicks running around in their new home.

I don't remember doing this, but I have been told over and over that when I was about 2 1/2 years old I took a 3 gallon jar and put lots and lots of chicks inside and somehow managed to put the cover on. I had no idea that baby chicks could suffocate, but I found out soon enough and my parents were none too pleased. I was a baby chicken killer. I just thought they looked so adorable all stuffed together in a jar which actually was the container that you would fill up with water and turned upside down on a trough. The water would seep out and the chicks would have fresh water at all times. Still to this day my dad reminds me of what I did 55 years ago. And yet he doesn't remember that I had called him just two weeks ago. The mind is a mysterious thing and I am still the baby chick killer.

We always had a fresh supply of eggs and we would go in and gather them every day, always surprised that the eggs were still warm sitting under the hens. We had a milking cow named Bessie and we all learned to milk her and I remember squirting the teats towards the cats coming to get their share and squirting milk directly from the cow into the cat's mouths, and we always set a bowl aside for them. We were just like the Walton's on Little House on the Prairie except their house was much nicer.

Castration days came every year when the baby bulls became steers in order to raise and sell them to a slaughterhouse, to be butchered and cut up and packaged and then sold in grocery stores to the general public. That was a very fearful day for me because we had a chute that we would have to get one of the baby bulls into and then have to flip it sideways so that the animal would stay still and could be castrated easily and quickly. Blood stopper and Lysol were put on the open wound so that it could heal without infection. I'll never forget the smell of that dark Lysol that was used to disinfect the steers before and after the operation and the bellowing and frightening sounds the animals made while they were being cut. But my dad was very matter of fact about it and taught us that the animals were there to provide food and nourishment for his family and others and although he did not take pleasure in it, that was his job and he needed to do it. That is what it meant to be a farmer and that was his life. We lived in North Dakota and even on the coldest days when it was -30° and the snow was 6 feet high my dad was out there feeding the animals and doing all the chores that needed to be done.

When it came time to butcher, the steer would simply be shot in the head, never feeling any pain. The animal was then hoisted up by its two back legs, it's neck sliced to drain out the blood, sliced down the middle from top to bottom when all the guts came pouring out. The smell was horrific and all the innards stayed in metal tubs. Almost every part of the animal was used; the heart, kidneys, liver, tongue, hooves, the whole head, and the intestines which were cleaned out, turned inside out, sterilized and used for sausage casing. That was true in particular for the pig intestines.

I can still remember the liver sausage and the summer sausage that we used to have for breakfast, lunch or dinner. There is nothing in the store as I can possibly compare to homemade sausage or the taste of free range chickens and steroid free beef. The thing is though, that since my early 20s I have not eaten red meat. I think my dad still has a hard time with that one. I wonder if that's where it started, my not being a carnivore; when I had to actually see and smell where the meat came from. Although I still do eat poultry it's no more beef or pork for me.

It was at the same time a very hard life and yet a very satisfied one. To be able to see where our food came from starting as a very tiny little seed and turning into a watermelon plant or to see a calf being born was an amazing gift even though I did not appreciate it at the time. Back then I just wanted to sit in my rocking chair and read a book. But being the child of farmers I did what I was told to do whether it be gathering beans from the garden for dinner or cleaning the barn which meant in fact shoveling shit, wheelbarrow by wheelbarrow and then laying down clean straw for the cattle who needed shelter in the winter. All that cow poop was then dumped into the manure spreader which Dad used to fertilize the fields where the alfalfa would grow once again in the spring. After that it would be time to mow it all down and make bales of hay to feed the cattle in the winter. And on and on went the cycle of life. Nothing went to waste.

Anything that was extra such as gristle, fat, bone, testicles, penises, kidneys and anything else not sold to the public in packages was transformed into other edible substances such as hot dogs, baloney, dog and cat food and various other goodies and put in the ingredient list as animal byproducts.

Recently, bull penises have become a very prized doggie treat wherein the penises are first twisted and then dried and come out sort of the texture of rawhide and is sold under the name of Bully Sticks which our little French bulldog, Joe, loves to high heaven. They are very expensive considering they are a byproduct but the brilliance of the idea of turning bull cock into a dog treat and marketing it to a very demanding public is pure genius and is one of those things that you think to yourself . . . Goddamn it! Why didn't I think of that?! Why didn't I think of twisting bull penises and selling them over the Internet? But whoever did think of that deserves a big pat on the back and a good crotch sniff from every dog who has ever had the pleasure of chewing on a dried up old bull dick. Yum!

To this day I hate to see anything go to waste. I believe it is integrated into my DNA and my children, having grown up in a different era think I am bonkers. Nonetheless, it bothers me when somebody puts something in the trash that should go in the recycling bin, and I use printing paper that it has already been printed on but is no longer of any use and I flip it over and use it to print out coupons or other things that are not necessary to be mailed. It's amazing the amount of paper you can save that way. I love metal art where people take pieces of scrap metal that would otherwise be thrown away and make something amazing out of it. And I have the greatest respect for restaurants that wrap up their leftovers and donate it to homeless shelters or food banks.

That's just one more reason why MS is such a shitty disease; because I used to be able to do so many things myself that now I have to pay a professional to do. My mother was the queen of making do, and I learned so much from her.

While I was growing up I had no idea what a strong woman she was. From the age of about 17 or 18 she started to feel fatigue, depression, and she stumbled a lot so other people just thought she was clumsy or just plain drunk. She was married to my dad when she was 17 while her symptoms continued to get worse after each child born. Still through it all she had six children and I am the second born. When things started to get quite serious she went to doctor after doctor and no one could figure out what was wrong except to say they thought it was psychosomatic and all in her head. My dad also thought it must all be in her head and took her to see a couple of psychiatrists which was devastating to her because she had no one to turn to. She even ended up getting a hysterectomy, the doctor thinking it might just be "woman troubles" and thinking that that would help her, but of course it did not. This was 60 years ago so much has changed since then.

When I was 21 and having already left home and married with a child of my own whom we named Lara, my husband Cheap Wad (not his real name) and I and baby lived in a fourth floor walk-up apartment in Brooklyn New York. One evening I got a call from Mom whom at that time I spoke to very often and she told me she had finally gotten a diagnosis and that she had MS. She was so relieved to finally know what it was that she was up against and that no one would any longer think she was crazy. When I think of it now and all the times when she would stumble and we as little kids would laugh at her, I am heartbroken because now the same things are happening to me and I know just how she felt and I am so very sorry.

I remember once in the middle of the day hearing her crying in her room and I went to her and sat beside her on the bed. I asked her what was the matter and she put her arms around me and said it wasn't us kids, that we had done nothing wrong and she was just feeling a little sad. I didn't know what to say or what to do and so I just left her alone. I'm sure now that she must've been thinking of her helpless situation and how things were getting worse and how depressed she was. She needed help but no one could figure out how to help her. Motherfucking MS. It changes who we are. It changes what we do and how we feel about ourselves and how we react to everything around us, to everybody around us, and especially to how we think about ourselves.

I have just turned 58 and am just now beginning to be able to separate my having MS from who I really am on the inside, my spirit, my being. I am finally able to see that having MS is not the end of my life and that there is so much I can do to help other people and impact the world in my own way because I do have MS. I am just concentrating on what I can do and not dwelling on what I cannot do.

My Mother had a very severe case of MS. My littlest brother was born when I was 16 years old so he really saw the brunt of what Mom had to go through and he helped her more than any of her other kids. We were grown and moved away and had families and children of our own. He lived with her through the worst of the disease and so he is one of my heroes and not only that but he is one of the funniest people you could ever meet. I very rarely see him but I think of him almost every day. I love my little Bro.

My dad stayed there with her through it all. She died just before their 50th wedding anniversary and after she died Dad said that no one could possibly understand the kind of love they had for each other; that young people who are just getting married and are so totally in love have no understanding of what real love is. He told me she asked him to help her to die and with tears streaming down his face he told her no, he just couldn't do it. And to this day he says he doesn't know if it was the right thing to do because she suffered so much.

Mom spent a lot of time in the hospital where everyone knew her and everyone loved her. She was really a very reserved and private person and very shy. There was one time when she had a grand mall seizure lasting over a half an hour and when she finally came out of that seizure she thought she was Dolly Parton! She was singing Dolly Parton songs and speaking in a Dolly Parton voice and flaunting her Dolly Parton cleavage. During those moments she made everyone so happy because it was so unexpected and so not like her and because it came out of nowhere. It was just really an honor to be a witness at my mother's debut. All of the staff came in to see her and interact with her and she even signed a few autographs. Later on, when she was told what she had been doing she was mortified and felt she had made a fool of herself but I think in those moments she really found herself, she found herself completely uninhibited and totally joyful and making everyone around her delighted. Unfortunately, that part of my mom that was Dolly Parton was never to be seen again.

Now, having MS myself I can't even imagine how she raised six kids, made all the meals every day, had a huge garden to tend to, did all our own canning, made enough jellies and jams to last the whole year, did all the baking. She made sure we were all up and had clean clothes to wear and ready to go to church on Sunday and ready for school every morning. Back in those days she had a wringer washing machine in the basement and no dryer so that all the clothes needed to be put into metal wash tubs, lugged up the stairs to be hung on the clothesline no matter what the season. She was a farm woman, a pioneer woman from pioneer stock and old world values living in the house that my Dad was born in.

I understand now her incredible frustration and anger about what life had dealt her and how she took it out on us kids with spankings and how we were made to kneel in the corner sometimes on corncobs with our faces against the wall. It was all too much for her and because Dad was always working outside to support our large family and he didn't have much time to help with the kids and most of it was left up to her. I just can't imagine being able to handle all of that and having a dreadful disease that she couldn't even put a name to. My heart has softened towards her since I started therapy. I wasn't even thinking about things from her point of view; I only saw things for my little girl point of view, living in the past and remembering the toughness of our lives and so now I have empathy for what she went through and I can forgive her.

At the time we were just little kids doing what little kids do, getting into trouble and being the little hooligans that we were and yet we worked hard too, doing our chores and helping with the farm work and in the garden and never realizing how poor we were. But now that I am grown and in an age where we have so many electronic and electrical devices to help in our everyday lives, I find it astonishing to see what she was able to do. And to top it off she very rarely complained about her life and we as children had no idea that she was so very sick.

And so now back to Uncle Tommy. As I stated before Tommy lived on the farm with Grandma and Grandpa and then he met Berta at a bar in a nearby town and everything changed. Tommy was very rarely there anymore and as kids we missed him so much and deeply resented Berta for taking him away from us. Her family owned a drive-in restaurant where the cars would come and park and waitresses would go out to them and take their orders. It was a local hangout place for kids and teens and families going out for a quick meal. For two summers I worked there and lived in Berta's parents' home.

I remember her dad as loud, obnoxious, mean and obstinant. Her mom was the ruler of the family and her word was the law. There wasn't a lot of warmth in their home. I stayed in an upstairs bedroom that used to be Berta's brother's room before he moved out. The room was cold and damp and stark and the only furniture was the bed, a small dresser and a bookcase full of strange German books, a few of them in English and because I was an avid reader I started to read these books.

These were very terrifying and strange books which told of Nazi torture devices and torturing women with broomsticks shoved into their vaginas and other terrible things that made me sick. I don't know why I never asked if they were books for research or books for a sadistic enjoyment or for a Nazi skinhead member to remember and study the genocide of millions of people inferior to his pure blood. I was just 15 or 16 years old and terrified by them and yet fascinated that they were just out in the open. Why would they put a young girl in a room like that? I never told anyone about the books or that I was very uncomfortable there. I hated it. I never felt loved or welcome. I felt tolerated and a means to a profit motive.

I worked long hours and never once saw a paycheck. One time Berta took me shopping and bought me some pretty clothes but that was it. I never said a word about it and just took it for granted that I was paid what I was worth. I somehow felt that I had to work there; that I had no choice; that no one missed me at home and that mom and dad felt better somehow that I was out of the house and was one less mouth to feed and take care of. I felt unprotected and put in a place where I did not want to be. I was very shy and scared but I was good at the job and never complained.

From a young age I learned to do what I was told and not to sass back so it was just natural for me not to speak up and even though I wanted to ask about being paid, I never said a word and never thought of quitting. I felt like I was farmed out and had no identity or value as myself and that I was always trying to earn my worth.

Neither Mom nor Dad made attempts to make sure that I was safe and happy and being treated honorably and neither one ever asked about my treatment or about my payment.

Berta's dad rarely spoke to me but constantly screamed at his wife and Berta but they didn't take any crap from him and they just screamed right back. What a dreadful man. What a dreadful family.

Eventually Tommy and Berta moved to Spokane Washington and had three kids who have all turned out to be very successful in spite of their troubled childhood; one of them is an FBI agent. They divorced quite some time ago and Berta took up with some guy who sexually abused her kids and Uncle Tommy got full custody, thank God. Berta eventually died of liver failure after years and years of drinking. She turned out to be a dreadful person who came from a dreadful family.

Aching for love, for appreciation and to be recognized, I had a crush on a really great guy who always talked to me as a friend and had a great sense of humor. He was much older than me; I think he was 21 or 22 at the time. He and his best friend came into the drive-in often which had booths and juke boxes and was a gathering place for a lot of young people.

One day Nate, my crush's best friend who was also about 22 years old asked me out, to see a movie that night and I accepted, of course, soaking up any acknowledgement no matter who it came from, although I didn't really like him a lot. He was crude and a troublemaker, but I agreed nonetheless to go out with him. He said he would pick me up at seven o'clock after he got out of work. I was excited and scared at the same time, being so naïve and needy and virginal. Which is probably why he asked me out in the first place; I have always been a magnet for men seeking naïve vulnerable women to exploit. I told Uncle Tommy and Berta about my date. They had no words of advice and no warnings or anything even though they knew him and his not being such a great guy reputation. I put on my cutest short set and put on a little makeup and did my hair and thought I looked cute and I was really psyched to go to a movie with a guy.

Seven o'clock came and went; eight o'clock, nine o'clock, 10 o'clock came and went. No words of advice from Tommy or Berta. Like, what a shithead, what a cad, don't go out with him EVER! But no one said anything, not a word. I just kept waiting. Not even a phone call.

Finally at 10:15 he came driving up in his bright red convertible, honked the horn and without even thinking about it I walked out to his chick magnet car, he actually got out of the car and opened the door for me . . . . bucket seats almost to the ground. After we said hi, I I asked him why he was so late and he told me he fell asleep when he got home from work and me, thinking we were just going to go to the late show, was disappointed when he said it was too late. He did not seem sorry or remorseful one little bit and I had a gut feeling that this was all staged. By this time we were already driving and he told me he would just take me for a drive. Well take a drive we did, about half an hour out into the middle of nowhere. I had no idea where I was when he stopped the car. We were out somewhere in the country with trees all around and not a building in sight. Now I was horrified and scared and feeling very stupid when it finally came to me that all he wanted from me was to fuck me . . . . No movie, no dinner, no getting to know me. Nothing but hump 'em and lump 'em and it also crossed my mind that this was some kind of a bet that he had made with someone that he could do me and that I would get a reputation as a slut.

Meanwhile, I had to pee so badly but I was afraid to get out of the car and pull down my pants out in the wilderness with the really creepy, quite capably a rapist and who knows what else in the car. I had no idea what this guy was capable of and I had gotten myself in this situation where no one knew where it was and even I had no idea where I was; in a very precarious situation with pretty much a total stranger.

He started to kiss me and put his hands all over me in a very demanding way trying to pull off my shirt but I was resisting and in the meanwhile I had already started to wet my pants and finally decided to tell him I had to go really bad so I headed for the nearest tree, took down my pants and peed with great relief and with great fear at the same time not knowing if he was going to come after me. By now my pants were soaked and I more than likely smelled like fried onions and greasy burgers and urine.

When I got back into the car I was humiliated for being such a baby and wetting myself but I realized later that the wet pants and the smell of pee may have saved me from being raped, ruining any fantasy he may have had about having sex with a virgin and that my guardian angel had been with me all the time. I told him I just wanted to go home. He was totally disgusted with me and did not speak to me all the way back to the Nazi house. I got out by myself, no door opening for me this time and slithered into the house sure that he could see my wet pants and the pee stain I had left in this beautiful Mustang.

The next morning I got up and went to work as usual. I don't remember anyone voicing concern about my "date" and I never said a word to anyone feeling dirty and stupid and ignorant and sure that soon everyone would know about what had happened or some version that he would make up and my reputation would be shattered. And most of all I was terrified that he would tell Trey, the guy I liked, and I would lose even his friendship and he would never want to talk to me again.

I had no one to talk to. I was so young and so naïve and I thought the whole thing was my fault. I was disgusted with myself and ashamed and felt like such a dummy to think that I had actually been grateful to that Possible Rape Wad. He had picked me up 3 1/2 hours late and I thought he would treat me like a lady and with respect and we would have a good time. All I wanted was to feel special and cute and fun to be with. What a God damn Shithead.

Why hadn't Uncle Tommy or Berta protected me, put their foot down as my guardians and protectors? Again, I just didn't feel worthy of love and protection. I only felt shame and humiliation and felt that I had sinned.

There were several times when Uncle Tommy and Berta took me to adult parties with them where there was drinking and couples making out and while they went to mingle with their friends I just stood all alone and finally found a place to sit down. Uncle Tommy brought me a can of beer and I just sat alone, drinking beer and listening to music. It was the first time that I ever heard Barbra Streisand sing. It turned out to be a very, very long night and I had several beers and probably made a fool out of myself. I don't remember much after that. Uncle Tommy and Berta sometimes even gave me beer after work in the drive-in. They actually thought it was funny when I got drunk. And these were my caretakers, the people who were in charge of my safety and my well-being. I never mentioned to anybody in my family about the bad influence they were on a very naïve girl. Add to this day, I hate the taste of beer.

More crap to stuff into my being and I was only 16. And yet there was room for much more to come; at least 42 more years and counting.

We are a family of secrets and I only know bits and pieces of what has all occurred. I grew up a lot during those summers and I became less shy, I lost a lot of weight, kept my virginity and stuffed all that shit that I saw and felt and l shoved those feelings deep, deep down.

Like I said, secrets in the closet. Some of those secrets in the Nazi's closet.

5

DASTARDLY DEBILITATING DISEASE

When people, as opposed to plants, animals or any inanimate objects ask me why I am in a wheelchair I let them know that I have MS; that is Multiple Sclerosis or as it is called by its more common name, Motherfucking Shit Disease. It is a neurological disease that tries to be very tricky by making the body think that there is a foreign body inside of us that it must attack. That is, an autoimmune disease, whereby the body actually sends its own defenses to try and fend against a threat that is not really there, making it, I guess, a delusional disease sensing things that are actually not there. Sort of like a ghost virus that your body must attack and so havoc is created.

Think of it like a video game which now that I think of it could be a game called MS: Attack on the Spinal Cord or perhaps Myelin Sheath Assault.

It does this by causing plaque deposits in the brain and spinal cord so that the nerve impulses cannot pass from one neuron to the next. That means when we tell our body to do something it won't listen or it will do something totally unexpected, unwarranted, and generally dastardly. For example legs will start to tremble uncontrollably, bladder control goes completely kaput, in the middle of the night you feel like you're being fucking electrocuted, or parts of your body go completely numb and are useless pieces of dead weight. And that's on a good day.

Many people feel various levels of pain, some of which are excruciating. I fortunately have only moderate pain since the meds I take to control the pain are working quite well. What I do have is goddam fucking paralysis of my left side and both legs, no fricking bladder control whatsoever so I use catheters, fatigue which is one of the main debilitating symptoms of MS and life altering shitty ass depression. My legs often tremble or seize up and it feels like an excruciating charlie horse.

I have several lesions on the right side of my brain and on both sides of my spine. Since the right side of the brain controls the left side of the body that is the side that has become paralyzed.

I have had relapsing-remitting MS since I was in my late teens and diagnosed when I was 22. That lasted for about two years and then I went for about 10 years with no MS symptoms at all. After the birth of my second child my MS symptoms started to come back again. At this stage of MS it is called relapsing remitting which means you may have an exacerbation of symptoms and then you get better again. However each time this happens some of these symptoms will stick with you and you must adapt your life to whatever level your disease has progressed to.

At some point, some of those of us with MS entered the stage of secondary progressive MS which means that we started with relapsing remitting but at some time and for some unknown frickin' reason we no longer relapse and are now in a period of having the disease progressively doing what it thinks it should be doing, as we, the patients (my voice recognition program just typed in patience) hah!!, are just trying to do our fucking best. And believe me that can be a goddamn mess.

There are drugs that can help the symptoms of MS but as yet there is no cure. I take pretty good care of my body using electrical EX-N-FLEX machines which are awesome and I highly recommend to stretch my arms and legs, by taking lots of supplements and vitamins and most of all by seeing a psychotherapist who bless her heart has helped me to see that I am not defined by my MS but can in fact learn many coping devices for my life in general and learn invaluable lessons from having MS.

By going very deeply, and looking very honestly at myself I have found strengths and talents and parts of myself that I never even knew existed and I have found the courage and strength to utilize them. Therefore I do not pity myself, I do not feel sorry for myself, I do not dwell on the negative, I face the obstacles that come in front of me one at a time knowing that there are spiritual forces beside me, within me, and all around me guiding me and helping me to live a life that has value and that I can share with others. There are however times when I feel like a pathetic little fucking wimp but then I can pull it together again and keep on moving on.

There is no drug that is as powerful as the inner spirit, the real self, the self that comes from cutting off the ego whenever it rears its ugly head and paying attention when it gets in the way and that my friends, is what the ego loves the best; to get in our way and show us who's boss. In reality the ego is our fucking enemy. Say it with me people, fuck the ego!, fuck the ego!; and one more time . . . Fuck . . . The. . . . Ego!!!!!!!

By writing this book I have truly slayed my ego on many levels because there are things within that are so demoralizing, humiliating, disgusting and traumatic that I never even thought I could talk about them . . . ever. And now I am putting it all on the line and hoping to show others the freedom that comes from just letting it go, just admitting our mistakes, forgiving ourselves and moving on so much stronger and wiser than ever before.

6

SHITTY LITTLE DITTY

You're just having a normal day, stacking the dishwasher or taking the clothes out of the washer and putting them into the dryer or cleaning up the dog's diarrhea because he ate something outside that he shouldn't have, or if you're a guy, maybe you were jerking off while your significant other was in the shower because you know you're not getting any tonight—she has her period and has been really bitchy all day long so you might as well take care of yourself so you can get a good night's sleep—or maybe you are tinkering with the lawnmower, and all of a sudden, a song will pop into your head and just won't fucking stop. It's stuck in your head like gum gets stuck in your kid's hair.

No idea where it came from, it's always some god-awful song and probably something you have not heard for at least fifteen to twenty years. Today, for me, it was:

> You are my sunshine, my only sunshine,
> You make me happy when skies are gray,
> You'll never know, dear, how much I love you,
> Please don't take my sunshine away.

Which by the way I Googled and found out that the original song was written by John S. Hurt in 1939, and became famous by Johnny Cash. Now I really am in the mood to hear Johnny Cash's music . . . hold on a sec. Ah, that's nice . . .

I mean, what the hell! I haven't heard that song since forever, and I was just organizing my coupons and that shitty little ditty shows up unannounced, uninvited, and totally unwelcome. Or like the one time when I was writing something for a therapy session and I mentioned the Kenny Rogers song "The Gambler":

> You got to know when to hold 'em, know when to fold 'em,
> Know when to walk away and know when to run.
> You never count your money when you're sittin' at the table.
> There'll be time enough for countin' when the dealin's done.

This one written by Don Schlitze in 1978 and I also found out that Kenny Rogers sang that song on The Muppet Show so it's no wonder I get that one on spin cycle in my head. Don't get me wrong, I love Kenny Rogers, but for the love of all that is holy, I couldn't get that godforsaken song out of my head for days. I'm not kidding! Days!

It happens to Lara, my daughter, a lot too, so one or the other of us will start a sentence by saying, "You know what song I've got stuck in my head?"

And generally, I'll have something I'm humming in my head also not even realizing it, and I'll say, "Is it 'Thunder Cats'?" which was Ryan's favorite TV show when he was just a lad. I would stop whatever I was doing during that time and sit down on the couch to watch it with him.

Of course she'll say, "No, it's 'Celebrate' by Kool and the Gang," or something, and then she will sing the whole frickin' song; it usually comes out of her when she's cooking. It is like a recurring nightmare, because she has that song stuck in her head only while cooking, which she loves to do, and I am really and truly sick of it. I never liked the song in the first place and then to have that song sung out of tune by a tone-deaf dingbat is just plain excruciating.

> Celebrate good times, come on! Let's celebrate.
> Celebrate good times, come on! Let's celebrate.
> There's a party going on right here, a celebration to last throughout the years.
> So bring your good times and your laughter too; we're gonna celebrate your party with you!

And she will go on and on dancin' and movin' and groovin' to the music, really getting into it. Just let me add that both Lara and I are among the one hundred worst singers in the entire state of Texas. Seriously, we are just that bad. Either one of us could very likely get on *American Idol* just by showing up at the auditions of the really atrocious performers.

I found out from reading an article in Wikipedia that the song is also notable for having played when the remaining American hostages returned home following the 1979-1981

Iran hostage crisis and then was rewritten in 1984 as the jingle for Diet Orange Crush. Pretty cool, huh?

So then we'll try to get the songs out of our heads by singing our respective songs to each other and just end up rolling in laughter with the other person's song now stuck in our heads.

I wonder what that means. Is it some sort of OCD or some brain malfunction, like with the old record players when the needle would get stuck, and it would play certain parts of the song over and over, until you actually got up off your lazy frickin' ass and fixed it? I wonder if there's an actual name for when that happens, like maybe stuckinyourheaditis or hemorrhoidalbrainmalfunction because it's such a pain in the ass, or maybe it's some very subtle way of your mind telling you to pay attention to something you are completely unaware of. For example "You Are My Sunshine" is my psyche telling me to pay attention to what makes me happy, because if I'm not happy, how can I contribute to anyone else's happiness? And "The Gambler" is perhaps telling me when to speak up and when to shut up, like that gorgeous Serenity Prayer by the theologian Reinhold Niebuhr so eloquently states:

> God, grant me the serenity
> To accept the things I cannot change;
> The courage to change the things that I can;
> And the wisdom to know the difference.

I mean, seriously, there's got to be something to this, because it happens too much to be an accident. I'm going to have to ask Dr. Cinzia about it when I next see her. Of course, the first thing that she'll say is "What do you think it means, Renae?" It will go around and around for a little bit, but eventually, I'll get an answer from her. And I'll pass it on to you because I'm sure that this fucking brain-fart dilemma must happen to just about everybody, or at least I hope it does. Misery loves company, and nothing is more miserable than a shitty little ditty stuck in your head day after day only to be replaced by an even more repulsive shitty song like "Tiptoe through the Tulips."

This brings me to a really funny story. When Fuckwad and I owned our antique store, a man came in one day; he was walking around and looking at things while Fuckwad and I were debating if he really was Tiny Tim or not because he was the spitting image. (Where did the saying spitting image come from anyway? Yuck!!!) I mean, this guy had that god-awful long, dark, stringy hair parted down the middle and that unforgettable pointy nose, and he just looked the part of the total freak that is Tiny Tim.

Now, mind you, these were in the good days when Fuckwad was not a Fuckwad; he was my husband and my best friend, so we just sat there giggling for a while. He finally dared me to go up to the guy and ask him if he was in fact Tiny Tim. Well, me being the gullible, ditzy person that I am, I gathered all of my nerve, stepped down off the podium, walked to the other end of the store, and asked him, quite sure that it really was him, "Are you Tiny Tim?" ready to welcome him into our store and maybe have a little chat with him.

But alas, alack, he just said, "No." Meanwhile, Fuckwad was laughing his ass off because there was nothing I could say to that really.

I think I said something like: "Wow, you look so much like him," and still he said nothing. It might have been a huge compliment to him, or I might have just insulted him like so many others in the past had. To be honest with you, I still think it was him; I mean, who really would want to be a Tiny Tim look-alike? Tiny left soon after that, and for several days, I could not get that godforsaken song, "Tiptoe through the Tulips," out of my head.

We had quite a few famous people come to the store over the years, including the Smashing Pumpkins. This was at the time when in their first album *Gish*, named after the famous silent film star Lillian Gish, had just come out, and they were going to be on the front page of *Spin* magazine. They had picked our consignment store in lower Manhattan as the location to do a photo shoot for the magazine. Ryan was about six at the time, and they asked him and his best friend Mark to join in some of the photos. And so it happens that Ryan and Mark are in the centerfold of the one-hundredth edition of *Spin* magazine with The Smashing Pumpkins, the whole bunch of them acting like little kids. And they even ended up buying some vintage guitars from us. At the time, we had no idea who they were or how famous they would become. They were just really nice, down-to-earth, friendly kids, and they were great with our son.

I wonder if they ever get stupid songs stuck in their heads. And you know what would be really great? If they wrote a song about it, about the pathology of getting the worst songs ever to play over and over and over again silently in your head until something else comes to take their place or you get sent to some rehab center somewhere that specializes in dumbass-song-stuck-in-my-head psychosis, or perhaps just-shoot-me-now addictions, because if there is such a place, then just sign me up. I wouldn't even need an intervention. I'd go willingly and embrace any help they could give me. Lara should really come too, but in her case, I think it would have to be an intervention.

7

PERSONAL ASSISTANT
TO A TRANSVESTITE MURDERER

For a period of about eight months, I worked as the personal assistant to Robert Durst, who seemed to be a very charismatic, high-energy real estate developer. At the time, in 1981, I had no experience in the real estate industry, but that did not seem to bother Mr. Durst. The woman I was replacing had worked for Robert for eight years and was now leaving because she was soon to have a baby. She had very little patience to teach me what I would need to know, and either because of her pregnancy or because it was just her nature, she was very terse with me. She really seemed to want to get the hell out of there. I really couldn't blame her.

To say I was winging it for the first several months would be putting it mildly. When I needed to take dictation for Robert, I scrambled like a jackrabbit trying to keep up with his very fast speech, and so there were many times when I couldn't even read my own writing and I would have to go and ask him what exactly he had said or wing it.

Robert Durst was nice enough to me. His expectations seemed quite low; he had me do mundane things, such as balancing his checkbook, calling his home to see if his wife was there—even though often he didn't even speak to her, he just seemed to be checking up on her—or ordering his lunch and making appointments. And then after I was there for eight months, Fuckwad and I decided to start a business of our own, so I gave my two-weeks notice. And it just so happened that at this time, Robert's wife, Kathleen, went missing.

Several days went by; Robert was rarely in the office and claimed that his wife was at their country home studying since she was in med school. And he said that was the last time that he had seen her or spoken to her. By now, the newspaper headlines were all about Kathleen Durst's disappearance and Robert Durst's possible involvement in his wife's murder. I had five more days to go before I was leaving this job, but things had gotten so unbelievably outrageous that I called in the next day and said I was not coming back. I mean, the guy was wacky and eccentric but to have been working for a murderer went way beyond my comprehension. I wanted no part of that fucking scary deal.

I've added some excerpts below as a summary of what a nut job he really is and the crazy things he did, including skipping bail and taking up an identity as a woman by wearing a long wig and women's clothing. You won't believe some of the things he did, and what's below is just a small part of the story. But here goes.

"Robert" Bobby Durst (born 1943) is a son of the late New York real estate mogul Seymour Durst and brother of commercial developer Douglas Durst, whom I saw every day when I came to work for Robert.

Durst reportedly witnessed his mother's apparent suicide at age seven when she either fell or jumped off the roof of the Scarsdale family mansion while her son watched.

According to reports, Durst underwent extensive counseling because of his mother's death, and doctors found that his "deep anger" could lead to psychological problems, including schizophrenia.

Durst went on to become a real-estate developer in his father's business; however, it was his brother Douglas who was later appointed to run the family business, which was reportedly worth about $650 billion. The appointment, in the 1990s, caused a rift between Robert and his family, and he became estranged. (and who among us would not fight his or her family for that kind of frickin' money? I know I would, for the love of god and all that is holy. I would even try my damndest to get him to fall in love with me . . . how hard could it be considering the incentive?. But then again . . . oh no . . . I might be dead by now. Murdered with a butter knife and a child's plastic scissors . . .)

In 1973, Durst married Kathleen McCormack, who disappeared in 1982. On December 24, 2000, Durst's longtime friend, Susan Berman, was found murdered execution-style in her house. Durst was questioned but not charged in both cases.

In 2001, Durst was arrested in Galveston, Texas, shortly after body parts of his senior neighbor, Morris Black, were found floating in Galveston Bay, but he was released on bail. Durst missed his court hearing and was declared the nation's first billion-dollar fugitive. He was caught in Bethlehem, Pennsylvania, after trying to steal a chicken sandwich and a Band-Aid, even though he had $500 cash in his pocket. A police search of his rented car yielded $37,000 in cash, two guns, marijuana, and Black's driver's license.

In 2003, Durst went on trial for the murder of Morris Black. He hired a well-known lawyer and claimed self-defense. Durst admitted to using a paring knife, two saws, and an ax to dismember Black's body before dumping his remains in Galveston Bay. The jury acquitted him of murder. (What!! Are you fucking kidding me?)

In 2004, Durst pleaded guilty to two counts of bond jumping and one count of evidence tampering. As part of a plea bargain, he received a sentence of five years and was given credit for time served, leaving him to serve only about three years in prison.

Durst was paroled in 2005. The rules of his release required him to stay near his home; permission was required to travel.

In December 2008, Durst made an unauthorized trip to the boardinghouse where he had killed Black and to a nearby mall. At the mall, he ran into the presiding judge from his murder trial. Because of this incident, the Texas Board of Pardons and Paroles determined that Durst had violated the terms of his parole, and he was returned to jail.

Robert Durst is pursuing legal action of his own in a fight over the family fortune. It's a lawsuit against his brother and a cousin. He says they're trying to stop him from naming his second wife as heir to his share of the family trust fund—reportedly worth millions of dollars a year (What?? Who in the world is this crazy lady who married him after all the shit he did? Talk about a sordid past!)

Robert Durst remains a millionaire under suspicion and under investigation on both coasts.[1]

Who says money can't buy a not guilty verdict? Here's a guy who had very good circumstantial evidence against him in the murders of two women and then pleaded self-defense in the murder of an elderly man, whom he chopped into pieces and threw in the river.

I guess you never can tell what someone is capable of unless you are in their inner circle. My local pharmacist could be a drug dealer for a major Columbian drug cartel. The lady who hoards felines doesn't even realize what that terrible stench is seeping out of her home. The local high school principal could be an embezzler, stealing hundreds of thousands of dollars meant for your children's education funds—which, by the way, really did happen in the small town of two hundred people in Hallefuckinlulah, North Dakota where I went to school. It seems that the school's bookkeeper really did embezzle $150,000 of the school's funding over the course of a couple of years. This was about ten years ago, and she pleaded guilty, making a deal to pay

---

1   **Mystery Of Robert Durst** February 11, 2009 Rebecca Leung February 11, 2009 (CBS)48 HR. Mystery

the money back and never spent any time in prison. Shortly thereafter, she moved out of town to God knows where and she is probably living a secret life as the vice president of a bank.

The local landscape artist could have human bodies buried under his thriving award winning plants and shrubs. The butcher at the local supermarket could be digging up bodies buried in the town's cemetery and putting the limbs, organs and other body parts in a giant food grinder and serving them as chopped meat or ground turkey to their unsuspecting clientele. And really, you might want to seriously think about what is in your takeout Chinese food. I've seen reports about New York City Chinatown restaurants that are serving dog and cat meat, and that is no lie because I saw it on *20/20* or one of those other news shows. I trust their sources implicitly. And everybody knows that dog and cat meat tastes just like chicken. I'm just saying.

So now you know I was assisting a transvestite murderer, and he seemed like such a nice guy.

8

MY VERY FIRST SPINAL TAP

When I was about twenty-one or twenty-two years old, I started to notice a fuzzy gray spot in my left eye that didn't go away.

It got to be quite bothersome, to the point where it was hard to see properly out of that eye and reading was very uncomfortable. I went to see a local optometrist, who sent me to a specialist to see what was going on. The doctor did a very thorough and comprehensive eye exam with lots of different tests. Finally, he sat down with me and my first husband, Cheapwad (there have been two) and with a worried look on his face, explained to us that what I had was optical neuritis. He said that if I noticed any other symptoms, I should immediately see a neurologist. I asked him why, and he said, "Just to be on the safe side." Back then I was so naïve it didn't even dawn on me to ask further questions of someone in authority. So when we left the doctor's office, I felt a little unsure and jittery and after 6 months, finally, the gray spot just disappeared.

The next thing I noticed was tingling in my left arm, which seemed to get worse as time went on. It was as if my arm had fallen asleep, but the tingling was so much worse than that. It became especially worrisome when I physically exerted myself in any way, and still I didn't say anything at all about it to Cheapwad. Having sex was becoming increasingly excruciating because of the god awful tingling. For at least three months, I tried to hide it, the tingling getting worse and worse and then finally, during one of our sexual encounters, I couldn't take it anymore. Cheapwad thought he had hurt me; I tried to explain to him with tears flowing down my face what I was going through. I had no idea what would cause something like this, but I finally made arrangements to see a neurologist.

I was admitted to the hospital for several days of testing. My hospital roommate was seventeen and a bundle of life; she was funny, adorable, antsy, and sick. She also had to go through a battery of tests, so we had a lot to talk about. It also happened that it was the same doctor who performed spinal taps on us both. She had already had hers done before I was admitted. I was already really scared even before she said her spinal tap was very painful, which made me dread the procedure all the more.

I mean a giant needle going into your spinal column was no day in the park.

My spinal tap was scheduled for the next morning, and I slept very badly, especially with all the hospital goings-on late at night and technicians waking us up to check our temperature and blood pressure and take blood samples at three or four in the morning. For the love of God, wouldn't you think they could do those things in the morning and let us just fucking sleep? And they wondered why we were so tired and grumpy in the morning. Assholes!

Anyway, the doctor was Indian and he seemed very caring and gentle. He reassured me that it would not be too bad and it would all be over soon.

I had on one of those horrible hospital gowns that opened in the back with just two little strings to tie together at the neck, totally exposing my back—and of course my ass which at the time was a little hefty.

I will from here on call this guy Dr. Ick. He had me lie on my side facing away from him in a special room for these special procedures. What I distinctly remember is the horrible color of the walls; it was like a dirty, dingy, puke green. Funny the things we recall when all is said and done even after almost forty years. He adjusted the bed just right so we could do what he needed to do: suck some of my life fluids out of me with that really long needle, which seemed to me to be at least a foot long and maybe even more.

It was very painful, but the worst part of it, even worse than the needle being stuck into my spine to take out several quarts of spinal fluid, was that Dr. Ick, while performing this delicate procedure was rubbing his cock against my backside. He had on scrubs, but I could feel his hard-on rubbing against my skin. I wondered if I was imagining this. Did he really need to have his body right up against me, and was he really dry-humping me while I had to stay perfectly still? I was facing the wall and could not see him, and I certainly was not going to say anything to him and risk being paralyzed for life or have him hurt me in some horrible way. I grew up a country girl in North Dakota, and I was very naive, so this was way out of my range of experience. The whole procedure seemed to take forever, and I wondered if he purposefully made it more painful than necessary to help keep control of the whole situation. I have had several spinal taps since then, and none of them have been nearly as painful. I believe the procedure now is to have a nurse present but that wasn't the case back then. No one looking in the door could see what he was doing because his back was to the door. He seemed to have set up quite a gig for himself.

Finally, he was finished—I mean with the spinal tap; I'm not sure if he ever came in his pants. I was told to lie straight on my back for at least eight hours or I would experience a devastating headache and to make no sudden movements, so I assumed that meant no pulling out a sawed-off shotgun and putting four or five blasts into his balls.

When I was wheeled back into my room, I was quiet for a long time. My roommate was out having more tests done. When she finally came in, she asked me how it went, and I asked her if Dr. Ick had done the same thing to her, rubbing his penis up and down on her while performing a dangerous medical procedure. She screamed, "Yes!" validating that he was not supposed to be that close to our exposed buttocks, not to mention sexually assaulting young women who are scared enough because we were sick. She said she hadn't told anyone either because no one would believe her. I felt the same way. I mean who would believe the two of us against a neurologist at a major New York City hospital?

When my dingle berry of a husband came to visit later that evening and I told him about the horrible incident, he did not believe me. I knew that he wouldn't. He said I must've just been imagining it, and when I told him that my roommate experienced the same thing, he was still very doubtful, so I knew there was no recourse for us. I wonder how many women Dr. Ick abused in this way, and I wonder if he ever got caught.

I knew then, and I know still, that Dr. Ick had humped me like a dog in heat while doing a spinal tap on me. I hope his prick gets hit with a major case of scabies and his balls develop oozing, pus-filled sores and then he gets an infected bowel and needs a poop bag and he has a really bad case of hiccups that just won't stop and all the symptoms of a terrible menopause and two ingrown toenails that hurt like hell . . . and oh yeah . . . I hope he gets bitten by a raccoon and gets rabies and has to go to the hospital where they discover his abhorrent behaviors from the past and after a very quick trial, he is sentenced to life in prison with no chance of parole.

That'll teach him to mess with vulnerable young women, who just want a diagnosis and not a perverted Dr. Ick putting his dick where it doesn't belong.

9

DEAR DAD

Dear Dad,

This is a letter I have wanted to send to you since I was three or maybe four years old, filled with things that I could never say to you in person, so here goes.

You goddamn, motherfucking, son of a bitch you egotistical, selfish, mean, crude, righteous, hypocritical, bastard cocksucker. You never even got to know your own children. We've all been afraid of you, you fucking creepy old man. We've all been afraid to speak our minds, to say the wrong thing, to do the wrong thing, to be the wrong thing—anything that doesn't fit your criteria; anything that would lead us to change or let us be creative or inventive—to be anything but just like you. You crazy ass, maniacal fuckhead. I'd say Fuckwad, but that's for someone else very special to me.

You treated Mom like your own personal maid/housekeeper/ cook/child-care provider/baby maker. She was someone who would bow to your wants and needs and cram all her frustration, hurt, pain, and disappointment way down to the tips of her toes.

Why didn't you show me love or respect me or praise me or tell me anything that was good about me? It was always about you, and you used your own kids to do what a hired man should do. We shoveled shit to clean the barn and carried fifty-five five-gallon pails of oats to the steers every evening even in the dead of winter. And we are talking about North Dakota winter. I'll tell you one thing, you unthinking turd for brains, I learned one hell of a work ethic—only I think I got that from Mom.

She worked like a horse even though she had MS since her late teens, and for so many years you never believed that she was truly sick. You thought it was all in her head. What a nasty thing to do to her—to make her think she was crazy. There are times when I feel almost nothing for you. I call you from a sense of duty, from expectation and guilt (and thanks for handing that down to me as well).

I dread talking to you on the phone. It's the same conversation all the time, and I still keep so much from you for fear of your disapproval. What's new, Dad? How are you feeling? What's new around town? You asked me if I remembered this one or that one and said that he or she had died. Of course, I never knew them, but we talk about them anyway. And of course, how is the weather? You ask about my kids, and I tell you the same thing every time: that they are both doing great and I will say hello to them for you. I send you gifts on every holiday and your birthday, always trying to please you with something new and different and unusual, still trying to gain your approval.

You guilt-inducing bastard, you never let me tell you my side, about my feelings and my true self. When I think of you now at the age of eighty-four, I think of a pathetic old man who alienates everyone he comes in contact with.

Now here I am at the age of fifty-seven, and I am finally working on finding and being the way I really am—who I really am and now you can't stop me. And the truth is, I am coming to understand you as well.

Well, Dad, on that note, I will sign off.

Your Loving Daughter, Renae

10

BLOODSHITPISSTEARSSWEATBILE

Confronting Fuckwad for his cheating on me just hadn't occurred to me; even though I dwelt on it twenty-four hours a day and got sicker and sicker with MS, depression, and unbearable grief, I was waiting for him to tell me that he was in love with someone else. Even after I had definite proof of his affair having seen his lover's letter to him on the computer screen and even after I finally saw those lies that were so blatant.

I just couldn't bear being unprepared for the consequences of his admittance. I asked him many times if he was having an affair, and he always denied it, saying in a belligerent and menacing way that I would be the first one to know. What a lying son of a bitch! What a mean, cruel bastard. I had been so beaten down by that time by the cruelty of his vile words and him beating me up verbally every single day, day after day after day after day, that I had totally lost any direction in my life. He had turned his family against me; he had turned my friends against me, and I felt powerless to face the future fearing I would lose Ryan, would have no place to live, and would not be able to find employment or a way to survive with my MS getting more and more debilitating and being paralyzed with depression.

Being so caught up in the nightmare of my life, I couldn't see my way to find solutions to even the simplest of my daily problems. I always had to have something to lean on in order to walk—walls, tables, furniture, people, and anything to give me stability. And then I finally got a cane, so I wouldn't have to rely on anyone to hold my hand or take my arm to get from here to there. I did my best to make sure Ryan attended all of his Little League games and school events and his acting classes, which he loved. But it was getting so hard to walk.

My bladder control was becoming worse and worse, so I often had to find a bathroom and struggle to get there, usually wetting my pants before I did. Embarrassment was my Siamese twin; it followed me wherever I went. I tried to hide it as best I could, but my best was not nearly good enough. I used sanitary pads, paper towels, napkins, and toilet paper, whatever I could find at the moment to soak up the urine that just seeped out of me beyond my control. I could never completely empty my bladder, so it would happen over and over again.

One of the most horrific events of my entire life happened in our store. Fuckwad was busy with a customer, and I was sitting on the raised platform that was our front desk so that we could see what was going on in the store. I knew I was in trouble. I had to go to the bathroom so badly, and I'm sure that my face looked tortured. It was about twenty-five feet to get to the twelve steps leading to the upper floor and then another twenty feet to the bathroom. To me, it was walking through the gauntlet. There were quite a few customers in the store, and everybody was busy.

Fuckwad finally finished with his customer, and I told him I was going to the bathroom. With every step I took, more pee would leak out of me, and even though I had stuffed my pants with paper towels already, they were soaked. And even worse than that, I was having my period, and I was feeling really sick. I walked all those steps to the stairs; I would put one foot on a stair and then the other foot, one foot on the next stair and then the other foot, counting them as I went up until I got to stair number twelve, and then I hobbled the next twenty feet to the bathroom where I was finally able to pull down my pants and sit on the toilet.

My panties were soaked with blood and urine and diarrhea had spewed out as I climbed the stairs. I just sat there stunned at how my body had betrayed me so massively and trying to figure out how I was going to get out of this horrific dilemma. I couldn't stop the tears. I couldn't get myself together. Snot was pouring out of my nose, and I used toilet paper as tissues. I took off my pants and put them beside me. I found some newspaper in the trash, which I put on the floor in front of me. I stripped off my blood-, urine-, and diarrhea-saturated panties and put them on the newspaper. I used toilet paper and paper towels, which I wet with cold water because there was no hot water up there, to clean myself off slowly, throwing the soaking-wet paper towels onto the newspaper along with my tearstained and snot-soaked toilet paper. I felt as though I was going to throw up; bile was rising up in my throat, and saliva began pouring out of my mouth. I spit it out several times and finally got that under control.

It looked like someone had been murdered right there at that very spot. My dignity was in shambles. My spirit was shredded. My body was weak, sickly, and diseased. I had no one to turn to and no one to help. I wanted to disappear. I wanted to die.

Finally, I dried my pants as best I could with paper towels, adding them to the mixture of putridness on the newspaper, knowing that I had been upstairs for a very long time. I washed and dried my face, brushed my hair, and somehow found the strength to go back downstairs and make my way back to the desk. Meanwhile, everyone downstairs was working, and I got busy at the desk doing what needed to be done.

It was about ten minutes later when I heard Brad from upstairs calling to Jeremy in a rather excited voice to come upstairs right away. Jeremy told him that he was busy and didn't have time. Two more times Brad called out to him, more and more heatedly, that he needed to come upstairs right away, so finally, Jeremy just gave in and went upstairs. I was rigid with fright, not believing what I had done—or rather not done. I knew at that very moment they were both staring at that whole bloodsweattearspissshitbile mixture that had come from every orifice in my body. For some reason, which I will never ever understand, I had just stepped over it and hadn't even cleaned it up. I literally had to step over that horrid mess to get out of the bathroom.

I heard nothing from upstairs, no gasps of horror, no screams of disgust or disbelief, but I knew they must be whispering about what to do. Should they call Fuckwad and show him, or should they just go downstairs and pretend that they had seen nothing? And thankfully, they did the latter because if they had told Fuckwad to come and see this monstrosity that looked like a pile of road kill . . . I can't even imagine the consequences. I just knew, I had no doubt, that it would be worse than anything I had ever experienced and just might be more than I could possibly bear.

How? How could I do that? How could I have been so oblivious and so not in the present that I would just leave that there for someone else to find? Had my depression become so deep and encompassing that it was taking over everything?

Was it literally taking possession of every part of my life? I was sick in every way possible—physically, mentally, and spiritually—and I had totally lost my way. Obviously, my subconscious was screaming for help, but there was no one there to help me and I couldn't see my way out of the eternal flames of this hell.

I had to do it. I had to take the torturous walk again, up the twelve stairs and twenty more feet to the bathroom, to see for myself if I really had done that, if I really had left that horrid mess right there on the floor in front of the toilet where I had to actually step over it to get out of the bathroom, not having any semblance of an idea that I hadn't cleaned it up first.

I saw what they had seen, but I can't imagine what they were thinking when they saw it. The garbage can was full, so I had to find a plastic bag to put that whole pile of stink into, which I did, sick to my stomach and sick to the very core of my being. I emptied the trash bag and my bag of bodily fluids into a larger trash bag, tied it up as best I could, and left it near the head of the stairs where someone would take it away. I went back downstairs one step at a time holding on for dear life to the rail. I went back to the desk and pretended that nothing had taken place, that everything was just fine and Brad and Jeremy hadn't just been witness to a horror movie scene where they'd just come across the carnage left behind by an unseen demon lurking in the shadows ready to pounce upon them as well. I shoved all that horror, humiliation, embarrassment, pain, sickness, weakness, and self-loathing as far down as I could possibly get it to go. No one ever mentioned it to me, and I wonder if and where Brad was ever able to pee.

I really wanted to disappear.

I really wanted to die.

11

CLUSTERFUCK RELIEF

Today, I finally got the call from Medicaid to make arrangements to have a state caseworker come to my home to evaluate my disability status and see what kind of help I am entitled to. To be honest with you, I dread this whole goddamned thing: a stranger in my home to help me shower, fix my meals, help me in and out of bed, do my laundry, clean my catheter supplies, etc. I never ever thought it would come to this, and I am scared, leery, and untrusting of any person who has free access to my home and my personal things, not to mention my naked body. I realize these people are licensed and bonded, but still, I am anxious and trying to work it out in my head as to how it's going to be. Since I am somewhat of an old biddy, I am set in my ways and my schedule, and now I will need to make changes to accommodate this unknown entity who will enter my life.

Dr. Cinzia has spoken to me about being careful to set rules, guidelines, and professional standards; being very conscious of keeping to those guidelines; and remembering that it is my home, that I am the boss and they are my employees, and that the aide is there to work around my schedule and not me to work around hers. Right, Dr. Cinzia, no problem. I got this covered.

This is very different from when I was in the hospital and needed a lot of care. As horrifying as that was, I knew it would eventually end and I could go home and have my privacy and as much self-reliance and self-respect as possible. I learned humility in the hospital and humbled myself to my caretakers, whom I got to know and appreciate during my eight-week stay in the hospital and their great physical therapy program. Of course, there were a couple of stinkers along the way, as there are in any herd of buffalo. The eight weeks seemed an eternity, but I worked really hard. They finally set me free, and ever so thankfully, I finally left the asylum.

This seems so different, so final—the loss of the control to which I have been clinging. I just do not want to be dependent upon and do not want to be naked in front of strangers. My body is hardly recognizable to me. I'm not what I used to be—a pretty woman with spunk, goals, and independence. No more. Only elderly people should need an aide. I am not ready.

My MS symptoms have gotten worse and I have gotten weaker. No matter if I'm not ready, it is time to accept the help to which I am entitled. I'm doing this partly for Lara because she worries so much about me since I am home alone most of the time. It has become difficult for both of us. She asks me how I am and all I have to say is "clusterfuck" and she knows I've had a rough time of it that day. And there is so much time and effort and work that she puts in just for me, which an aide should be doing instead.

It will make all of our lives easier so I am glad I finally took the plunge, scary as it is. It is for my own safety and quality of life and also for those of Lara and Brian, our roommate. They both work full-time and often overtime. They are my heroes.

Every day in the hospital they were my visitors—in the mornings before work and nights after work—and they always brought me something, my favorite being Starbucks coffee in the morning. I don't think they will ever know how much it meant to me to have their loyalty and love. They had the ability to make me laugh and not take things too seriously, even when they helped to change my soaking-wet clothing or do other disgusting things. They would be making faces, and we all would crack up laughing.

I know it's time to do this. It is necessary, and I trust that my life will be better because of the help. I pray that the right person will be sent to me. I will work at not being frustrated when I can't explain what it is that I need or how I want things done, and I will work on not being testy when I just want to be left the fuck alone. I will give it up to God and the powers that be to make this a positive healing experience. I will have more energy, my personal things will be taken care of, and I won't ever again spill a catheter container full of urine all over the floor and rugs and have to clean it all up with one hand and in a wheelchair and then do a load of laundry and deodorize and sanitize everything. It takes an immense amount of time and energy to do all that, which is just one of the utterly exhausting clusterfucks of which I speak.

So in reality, my aide will be a clusterfuck deterrent, which sounds so good right about now, because I just dropped a full bowl of shredded wheat on the floor and there is broken glass and milk and shreds of wheat all over the goddamn place. Motherfucking shit fuck! Why, God, why? Okay, calm down, Renae. You're on the way to getting some help, and it will all work out. It will only make things *better*. Meanwhile, I have to go clean up this latest damn mishamagosh.

12

A DARKER SHADE OF RAY

Preface to Shady Ray

My mother died eleven years ago. That was the last time I saw any of my siblings—three brothers and two sisters; it was not exactly a happy occasion on which to have a family reunion. I speak on the phone with my sisters, Jocelyn and Rochelle, but not with my brothers, and I know that none of us keep in touch with any of the others, so needless to say, we are not a close family in either proximity or family ties. We are scattered all over the United States, and although I know we would all like to keep in contact and be a close family, it just seems that when you let it go for so long, it gets easier and easier to let it go a little longer. That's eleven years of a little longer, and it seems like just yesterday.

It was a stunning telephone call I received two weeks ago. It came from my brother Ray, whom I write about in the story entitled "A Darker Shade of Ray," which follows this prelude. I was completely surprised to hear from Ray, and yet looking back on it all, it seems to fall into place since he was really the one remaining person for whom I had felt any resentment or with whom I had any unfinished business. I felt great trepidation knowing that someday he would read what is to follow and not knowing what the repercussions would be. I have confronted all of my demons, and now they attack me only once in a while; yet, at this time, my demon Ray was still snarling and digging his claws into me, still causing me harm, and I wasn't able to shake him loose.

And then he called, and as soon as I heard his voice, the darker demon dissipated, and in an instant, I was free of the past. I realized that I was the one who was clinging to the past and keeping the sharp talons of victimhood attached. I was the one feeling the weight of dragging that burden around with me day after day after day after endless day for fifty-plus years. Even though I wasn't aware of it consciously, it still weighed on me heavily. Getting rid of those shadows that didn't really exist in the present moment was like a lightning strike that just burned away and cauterized all of the old hurt, resentment, and open wounds that had never healed. Now we had a chance to start a new relationship, my brother and I, which was why he called me in the first place. It seemed that he, at the age of sixty, and I, at the age of fifty-eight and a half, were in similar places, taking actions to slay the dragons and get on with it.

The conversation lasted but fifteen minutes or so, and we got right down to business, no small talk, no chitchatting about the weather, no wasted words. We spoke of growing up with our hard-ass father and about how we had both now forgiven him his brutish manner and his inability to move from his righteous point of view. We both saw that he had many demons of his own to slay. And we spoke of how we both felt like the black sheep of the family, and we argued about which of us was really the blackest and

71

eventually agreed to share that unwanted title. We talked about how we both stopped going to church as soon as we left home right after high school graduation.

I told Ray about the time when Mom and Dad came to visit me, my first ex-husband, and our little girl Lara when we lived in Brooklyn. We lived in a neighborhood that was a little shady. I had not gotten the nerve or the stones needed to have an honest conversation about my religious beliefs. Being raised as a staunch Catholic and having parents who expected us all to go to church every Sunday and say the Rosary every night, I was scared shitless about how I was going to handle the church issue. Mind you, I was twenty-three or twenty-four years old at the time and still terrified of my parents' reaction to my not doing things exactly as a good Catholic girl was expected to do them. So I got out the old phonebook and found the nearest Catholic Church and the time of their Sunday services. I made up some lame excuse about why ex-husband number one and I would not be going to that particular Mass and sent them on their merry, dressed-up-in-their-Sunday-finery way.

Mom and Dad came back about an hour and a half later and told me that the entire religious service was in Spanish and they hadn't understood a word. I wanted to die. I was horrified beyond belief and had to do some fancy tap dancing to get my footing back. They said it was okay and the preacher was very nice and welcomed them; it just reminded them of the old days when Mass was said in Latin and they didn't understand a word then either.

I pictured them amid a whole congregation of people who were different shades of brown and from different

Spanish-speaking countries. They had hardly ever before seen people of color. Holy Mary Mother of God and all the saints in heaven, what had I done? "Thou shalt not lie. Honor thy father and thy mother. Thou shalt not take the name of the Lord in vain." I was going to hell in a hand basket. Talk about guilt! If I were a churchgoing person and had gone to confess my sins, my punishment would have been a lot more than the regular Our Fathers and Hail Mary prayers. It would have been many acts of contrition, praying with the Rosary beads, and possibly being beaten around the head and shoulders with palm leaves to erase the damage I had done to dirty my soul.

Ray laughed his ass off at that story, and I laughed right along with him, which I wasn't able to do for at least fifteen years after the whole incident. It certainly did not seem funny at the time.

At the end of our conversation, Ray and I promised to keep in touch. A week later, Ray called again to my astonishment, and we shared more of ourselves, being more real than we had for the last fifty-five years. I told him about the book I was writing, and he asked if I would please, please, please send him a copy to read and promised that only he and his wife, Meredith, would read it.

After you read the next chapter, you will understand why I balked at the idea of sending him my then unedited book. I told him there was a chapter about him in the book, and I promised to send it anyway no matter what the content. I needed to write this preface, Ray, so that you will read about my unfinished business with you knowing that it no longer presses hard on my heart and that I no longer need to hold onto my past to be who I am today: a potty-mouthed heathen with a hand basket attached to my wheelchair.

A Darker Shade of Ray

Well, Ray, I have no idea what to say to you. I don't know where to start, and I don't know where this will end. First things first, I don't like you. We hardly ever see each other, and still, I have always been seeking your approval, to no avail. You have paid no attention to me and the few times that I tried to connect with you, I have been ignored. The last time we saw each other was at Mom's funeral when you certainly let me know who was boss. I had spoken to Fuckwad on the phone; he wanted me to come home early, and I was upset. I was trying to tell everyone that I had to leave, but it was not because of my own desire to go but because my husband said that he needed me back home.

Perhaps I did act and sound inappropriately under the circumstances, but what is inappropriate when you are grieving for your mother and for your father and needing to spend time with your siblings? I was torn in half, and you, in your typical righteous manner, told me I should go and apologize to Dad because he had just lost his wife of fifty years and my behavior was adding to his stress.

I felt shamed and belittled. I felt shamed for the way I had acted, and I felt belittled by you letting me know that I was being selfish and was not being a good daughter. Fuck you, you righteous arrogant prick.

I did go to Dad and told him how sorry I was for my behavior and how sorry I was that I had to leave earlier than expected. Dad and I hugged one another, and he told me it was okay. We cried together for a while and went back to the rest of our family. Why did I feel the need to let you know that I had spoken to Dad and apologized for "making a scene," as you put it?

Your reply to me was: "You don't have to tell me that you apologized to Dad; that was between you and him."

Again, you were belittling me and making me feel about three inches tall. Why? Why did I feel the need to let you know I did what you thought I should do? Why did I need your approval? I just slithered away like the slug that I felt I was, as I said to you, "I just wanted you to know."

Yes, you pig; you are the close family member who tried to get Rochelle and me to have sex with you in the haystack. Yes, you bucket of puke; it was you who tried to put your hands into Rochelle's pants while the whole family was sitting around watching television. She dug her fingernails into you so deep she made you bleed. You always did hate her long fingernails, but I'll bet not nearly as much as she hated you for your incestuous actions toward her. She never told anyone what you tried to do to her sitting there in the living room until just recently when she and I were talking about you. She told me all about it. You fucking piece of shit.

I have been having dreams of you lately. You were angry at me, and you were trying to keep my mouth shut so I could not talk about "it," whatever it was. And in the dream, you were domineering and standing over me. The only recollection I have of your incestuous nature was in that haystack when you tried to fondle me and I just ran away and never told anyone. I know there is more that my subconscious is not ready to release, and I know I am getting closer to the truth. I want to know everything. I want to be free of you, in my thoughts, in my dreams, in my not knowing.

One of the most vivid memories I have of you was when you were about nine years old or so and the three of us girls—Rochelle, Jocelyn, and I—heard you yelling to come and help you in the grove of trees behind our house. I remember Rochelle and I came upon a scene that is forever etched in our minds. You had gotten two pieces of wood and nailed them into the shape of a cross, and you were nailing a cat onto the cross. One paw was already nailed all the way through; the cat was on its back, and you were nailing its second front paw using a big nail and hammering it, pounding it straight into that poor creature.

I'm sickened and nauseated even now thinking back to that moment in time with that poor animal tortured and screaming in pain and fear. You asked Rochelle and me to help you hold down the cat so you could nail the other paws to the crucifix. I remember being so horrified and disgusted by what you were doing, I was transfixed for a moment not believing what I was seeing. Then Rochelle and I ran away and told Dad what you were doing.

I don't remember anything about it after that; I don't have any recollection of what your punishment was; I wasn't there when Dad caught you crucifying a cat. But I do know that every now and then, as we became adults, Dad would bring it up as though Rochelle and I were somehow involved, but we made it perfectly clear that we had run away and had had nothing to do with that heinous act. And Dad said he knew. And yet he still brought it up. I wonder why.

Last night, lying in bed thinking about how I wanted to dream about you again, even if it was scary or uncomfortable for me, I remembered another incident—you fucking creep. Rochelle had a pet turtle that she kept in a metal washtub, and she fed it vegetables and took care of it every day. For some reason, I don't remember why, you were mad at her or something and you felt the need to get back at her, so you put her pet turtle, Shelley, in front of the wheels of the pickup truck and drove over him, crushing his shell and killing him instantly. Another notch in your belt, eh, brother of mine? Motherfucking cat and turtle killer, abuser of sisters and God knows who else with your arsenal of control and fear and intimidation.

I'm wondering if all of your perverted thoughts and actions are what keep you acting so righteous and arrogant, so that you can keep an upper hand in the situation even to this day when I am fifty-eight and you are sixty years of age. You've retired as a mechanic and now follow in Dad's woodworking footsteps, making wooden rocking horses for little kids. Well goody, goody for you! Aren't you just a chip off the old block?

It makes me wonder if you are one of those guys we hear about on television, when the neighbors say, "He was such a nice man; they were a nice, quiet family, a pillar of the community, and he made such beautiful rocking horses" and meanwhile the authorities are digging up bodies under your basement workshop where you keep all your tools and rocking horses ready for sale. Isn't that how it always starts with serial killers—torturing animals and molesting little girls?

Yes, Ray Wad, I know in my gut, I know within the deepest recesses of my mind that you did more to me than just what I remember, and so now, brother, I no longer seek your attention or your approval, and I know someday I will remember everything and then I will be free . . . of you.

I only pray that you've never hurt anyone else the way you hurt Rochelle and me and that poor dear cat. You, who are so nice and normal on the outside, are hiding a beast within: the Rocking Horse Killer. It sounds like an episode from my favorite TV show, *Dexter*, doesn't it? Maybe I will write to them and suggest it as a plot for the next season. I could write at least two of the episodes, because I have lived them, and they could say: "Based on a true story."

13

HOSPITAL BEDS AND CATHETERS AND WHEELCHAIRS . . . OH MY!

It is so frustrating to have to wait until other people are ready to do what I ask them to do because I can't do it by myself. MS is a bitch on steel wheels. Christmas packages are ready to go, but neither Lara nor Brian is ready at the time to take them to the post office. Think, think, think! What lesson can I learn from this? Patience, perhaps? Letting go? Give it up to a higher power? Trusting that it will get done and if it doesn't happen now it will happen later? Frustration and impatience solves nothing? Look at things from their perspective? Be gentle with myself? My angels and spirit guides will help me—they always do—and now I can let go of all that shit and read a book about a Holocaust survivor. That kind of puts it all in perspective.

I put off getting help around the house or even physical therapy because I just don't like anyone in my house helping me except my family, but it really is time. I don't trust people like I used to. The one person I trusted more than anyone lied to me, cheated on me, broke my heart and my spirit, and verbally and emotionally abused me, and now it just seems as though spontaneity is dangerous. I hate talking on the phone; I don't reach out to meet people or make friends. It just seems too exhausting; just taking care of me doesn't leave room for the unexpected, although when people come over with Brian or Lara, I am cordial and friendly and do my best to be "up." I feel that I need to be entertaining and to show an interest in what is going on around me even though many times I would much rather do something else, like read or take a nap.

I can't even imagine having another relationship. First of all, I am a lot of work. My body is weak and flabby and uncontrollable. I have to use catheters, and, good grief, who would want to have to deal with that mess? Or with hospital beds and special toilet and shower seats? I have fallen too many times to count, and I need help getting in and out of bed, on and off the toilet, in and out of the shower. Yes, it is definitely time to get a home health aide. Not exactly the kind of relationship I was hoping for. It's another chapter in the ongoing saga of lessons learned about knowing when it is time to give up ego-based barriers and relent. MS is one hell of a teacher.

What I miss about having a partner is the talking, sharing, hugging, kissing, and cuddling—all the sweetness of being with a man. I love sex. I just can't imagine how I would find someone who would want to take on all that. I believe that there is someone out there with a very special spirit that would match mine, and when the time is right for our spirits to collide, it will happen. I suppose I have more lessons to learn, mountains to climb, and therapy sessions to go to before something so wonderful will happen. Until then, I will start with an aide.

The next best thing to a real live man is that awesome vibrator that Dr. Ruth endorses in the Dr. Leonard's catalog. Good God! The thing is that you will need to set aside some private time because believe me when I tell you, from my own personal experience, that your orgasms won't stop and plus I don't have much private time any more. Or if you are lucky enough to have a partner who is not threatened by electrical devices that can give better orgasms than he or she can, you can use it together and have double the fucking fun! I just want to give a very loud shout-out to Dr. Ruth because that woman rocks!

I thought that Fuckwad and I would be together no matter what happened to either one of us; I believed our kindred spirits and senses of humor would get us through anything. I really thought that even when I started getting weaker and slower and began using a cane. But instead, it was the beginning of the end. Boy, did he have me fooled! His marital vows came to nothing but "until my wife's disability do we part."

I remember ironing his clothes, cutting his hair, even shining his fucking shoes, and packing all the new shit he bought to impress another woman (maybe even women) because he told me he had a great business opportunity in Minneapolis. He told me about it in such great detail; I fell for it hook, line, and sinker. I believed in him so much. I kissed him good-bye and told him how proud I was of him. While he was away taking advantage of this wonderful opportunity I took care of our son and our business, working with our employees, who probably knew the real reason he was gone.

Eventually, I learned that I had cut his hair and gotten him all ready and looking fine for his trips to see his lover in Dallas, Texas. They say that the wife is the last one to know. I missed all the blatant signs. Someone could have been walking back and forth in front of our store with a neon sign saying, "Fuckwad is cheating on you! Fuckwad is cheating on you!" flashing those words over and over, and I would've just walked right on by not even noticing or maybe laughing a little never thinking the sign was pointing at me.

It had to be someone else's Fuckwad, because my loyal and loving husband would never degrade and make a fool of me so deeply and cruelly and selfishly. We were a team, for the love of God and all the saints in heaven! I worked just as hard as he did to start our business. We were able to start a business with six thousand dollars that I got from a lawsuit. (I bit into a piece of metal machinery that somehow found its way inside my sandwich at a local fast-food restaurant.) Maybe it was my loving husband's way of trying to get rid of me . . . guess I'll never really know. (Just kidding . . .)

We lived for eight months on the second floor loft of the store, with mice running around, just a mattress on the floor, no hot water, and no way to refrigerate anything. We took showers in our friend's bathroom in his loft right next door to our store, and our little seven-year-old boy lived with us like that, all of us sacrificing to make our dream come true like squatters in a crack house. How could he forget all that? How could he forget that I was just as much a part of that business as he was and I loved it and I loved *him* so much I would've gone to the ends of the earth for him?

More and more, he told me I was not needed at the store, and still, I didn't get the message. I didn't understand it until later when I found out that his girlfriend had come to New York several times and actually came into the store so he could show her what he had built, what a big man he was, how smart and successful. He took her into the store with our employees there, so they all knew. Fuckwad expected them to live by the man's code of honor: a man never tells the wife when another man is having an affair. I wasn't aware of such a code until Fuckwad informed me about it after one of our employees told me about his cheating ways because he couldn't stand to see me so depressed and sad all the time.

Fuckwad just had to make somebody else the bad guy instead of taking ownership himself for the whole fucking mess. He needed to deflect the blame onto another, and I was the biggest deflectee of them all. A code of honor, *my ass*! He gave his lover gifts from our store, literally stealing from our family to make himself the hero. They spent the night in hotels while she was here and in Dallas. He told me he was meeting with his business partners and would be gone for a couple of days.

It meant still more money coming out of our limited family resources. He was taking her to restaurants while I searched for spare change in the couch to make ends meet. The phone bills to Dallas were astronomical; again, he was stealing from our little family. He bought himself a wonderful new wardrobe while I wore the same old shit because we were putting every cent back into the store, sacrificing, building equity, building our life together and our future. Goddamn bullshit. Motherfucker! Prick! What kind of code of honor was that?

I can't even imagine what he told her about me to make me seem so utterly pathetic and useless and crazy that he would be the one who needed comforting and solace and love. He set it up so that he could jump right into her life with our son while she supported him until he found a job. Meanwhile, I was left with nothing. I did not take one single thing from the store when I left to go to a city I had never been to before; I had no money, no car, and no job. My beautiful son was living with them while they built a life together and I built my life alone, starting from scratch—just me and my MS. BFF.

I wish that I had walked into the store one time to see them together, but I guess the universe had other plans for me. Maybe it was protecting me until I could absorb the treachery a little at a time until I was ready; it allowed me to do things at my own pace while my mental power was slowly building, and I just couldn't take it anymore. Physically I was damaged goods and getting worse all the time.

Okay. I'm going to go read for a little bit . . . *Man's Search for Meaning*, by Viktor E Frankl and think about what I have learned from these experiences. Reliving the pain really. Nobody said that therapy was going to be easy. But this is fuckin' ridiculous! I will steer my wheelchair into my bedroom, take my catheter to the bathroom, dump it out, and clean it with vinegar, and then I will transfer myself from my chair to my hospital bed, which in itself is not an easy feat. I will next work to get my catheter into the correct hole, because it gets a little complicated down there in the nether regions and sometimes it takes a lot of trial and error to get that tube into the pee hole and not the fun hole.

That's finally done, and now I need to get my body situated comfortably, my left side being paralyzed. I need to put two pillows, one on top of the other so that my heels don't touch the mattress because that burns. I need to sleep on my back all night long so that goddamn catheter does not get pulled out—that has happened too many times to remember, and the repercussions are really icky. And, oh yes, I forgot, before I get into bed, I have to take about eight pills, drink lots of water, and make sure there is a water bottle beside me because the medication makes my mouth so dry that it actually gets glued shut and I have to drink water five or six times a night just to be able to sleep. So yeah, what lesson must I learn from all this shit? That's for another chapter, because right now, I'm just too damn fucking tired to even think about it.

14

SOMETHING TO CRY ABOUT

I feel like a traitor, as though I am betraying her, being disloyal to my mother.

I feel a lot of guilt for not keeping in touch with her nearly as much after my first marriage ended and my relationship with Fuckwad began. It was partly because whenever I called Mom I had to speak to my dad as well, and he and I have had an uncomfortably distanced relationship ever since I can remember.

When I divorced husband number one, my father disowned me. No daughter of his would be such a tramp and take up with another man while she was still married, and divorce was not an option because the Catholic Church frowns upon such things. To make things even worse than they were, husband number one called my parents and told them that I was having an affair, making sure to alienate them from me. I knew it was wrong. I knew I was a sinner.

I had strayed from being a good little Catholic girl, which was what he had married, into a woman with hopes and dreams of her own. I was married at the age of nineteen. I was much too young and much too naive to pull away from everything I knew. Cheapwad was in the air force and stationed in Grand Forks, North Dakota, and I was going to college at the University of North Dakota when we met on a blind date. I was enthralled with him; he was from *New York City*, while I was from the middle of Nofuckingwhere. I was thrilled and enchanted that someone like him could fall for someone like little ol' me. He seemed so worldly to me. I was still a virgin and didn't give it up until we had been together for eight months. Even his best friend wanted to know what the hell was wrong with me. Finally, one night, on campus, when we were outside sitting on a bench with no one around, I gave him a hand job, and this ritual continued for about a month until he finally persuaded me to blow him. At that time, I thought it was disgusting and I really hated doing it, especially out in the open. I certainly was not going to swallow.

When I say Cheapwad, I am not kidding. The first time we actually had sex, it was under a blanket in one of the campus park areas, at night, with people intermittently walking by us. I couldn't wait for it to be over because I was sure that someone had to know what we were doing under that blanket. It wasn't good for me; he was not a good lover. There was no romance, and I was certainly not into having sex in public places, but I did it to please him, not believing that I deserved to be treated like a queen, like a woman of value, as though I were special.

I was just so happy that he or anyone paid attention to me, not even once thinking that he should take me to a hotel or someplace private and indoors where we could make love as lovers should, taking our time kissing and touching and feeling one another instead of just trying to get it over and done with quickly so we wouldn't get caught. We had sex like that for a long time before he finally saw fit to book a motel. I never said a word and to be honest never even thought about it, because I didn't think of myself as worthy of better treatment. Is it any wonder that I did not learn to enjoy sex for many, many years? He was just really not a very sensual man, and I was oblivious. Meanwhile, when we finally got married and moved to Brooklyn, New York, culture shock hit me like a mud slide.

I got pregnant almost immediately, and we were so afraid to tell his mother that we went to her beauty salon where she was under the dryer to tell her we were having a baby. Being a loud Italian woman, she screamed at us right there in public, "What? You *couldn't wait* to have a baby? You just got married, and now look at ya . . . no money, not even a pot to piss in and already you're pregnant!" We hung our heads in shame and slunk out of there having had any joy or excitement about having a baby slapped out of our stupid little faces.

When Cheapwad had his bachelor party given to him by his buddies in the Air Force, one of the gifts that they all pitched in to buy for him was a gross of condoms—not that the condoms were gross but there were 244 of them. There was just one little hitch: they had poked a pinhole in one or two of the condoms, and nobody knew which they were. Hah, hah, hah! Those guys were a laugh a minute, and with friends like that, who needed a diaphragm? Oh well, boys will be boys, and obviously, the air force had still not made men out of them. As the old proverb goes, you can lead a man to a dictionary, but you can't make him think.

For the first three months of our marriage, we had to live in his mom's small two-bedroom apartment. She called me a country bumpkin, which I was, but it was still an insult. I hated living there. I was scared to death of his mother, the Italian shrew, the you-are-not-nearly-good-enough-for-my-son, hell-on-wheels, motherfucking mother-in-law.

To say I was terrified to be away from Cheapwad would be an understatement. I went with him when he went to job interviews and waited for him in the lobby. It did not take long for him to get a job working for AT&T, and after those three months trying to hide among the shadows, we were finally able to move into an apartment of our own. Hallelujah! It was a four-story walk-up, but it was our four-story walk-up.

Meanwhile, I was a stay-at-home, agoraphobic, fish-out-of-water, pregnant, naive woman terrified to be out of the apartment by herself; I was a country fucking bumpkin.

One time, Cheapwad and I were in Manhattan for some reason or another, and I was dressed in a pretty sky-blue dress that showed a bit of cleavage. Cheapwad went into a store to pick up something I stayed outside on the sidewalk to wait for him. People were milling around, the sidewalk filled with activity, when a very good-looking man in a suit came up to me and asked me if I wanted a date. I told him I was married and waiting for my husband, feeling flattered that he found me attractive.

When I told Cheapwad about it upon his return he was horrified; he had to explain to me that the man thought I was a prostitute and that he was asking me to be paid for sex. I could've died right then and there from shock and horror! I had no idea about any of that—that a man could just come up to a woman and ask for sex! Right there on the street, right on the sidewalk, right near Macy's! I felt cheapened and so terribly uncomfortable with myself, and I felt that I had somehow done something inappropriate to cause that guy to approach me. Cheapwad did nothing to allay my fears. It just made me cling to him all the harder. If I'd known then what I know now, I would have asked that man if his wife knew what he was doing and told him to go take a long fucking hike. That goddamn shithead actually thought I was a streetwalker!

And I'll tell you something else, if I did decide to be a prostitute I would certainly would not be a streetwalker. I would have private clientele in a swanky hotel and charge an outrageous fee for the same reason I use Preference by L'Oreal—because I am worth it.

Which reminds me, it's time to color my hair. The gray is starting to show yet again.

Little by little, I gained some courage and walked the twelve blocks to the nearest library. I found myself a sanctuary. I loved going and I loved coming back with as many books as I wanted or as many as I could carry. I started reading everything I could on pregnancy, childbirth, and child care. I read books on breast-feeding and books by all of the leading women's rights advocates and started my awakening. As self-conscious and shy as I was at that time, I made decisions about how to have our child delivered and how she should be raised. I insisted that we go to natural childbirth classes, and surprisingly, Cheapwad relented on all of the decisions I made about and for our daughter. Even when we divorced, he didn't fight for custody, saying that I was much better at raising her than he was, which was the goddamn truth.

The childbirth class that we went to was run by a woman with five or six kids; the youngest, who was almost five at the time, was still breast-feeding. Honest to God, while she was teaching that kid would just walk up to her, lift up her shirt, and while he was standing there, he would suck on her breast, neither one of them showing the least bit of shame or paying any attention to the reactions of anybody else around them as she continued to conduct her class. It was awesome to see—a woman who really didn't give a shit about what anybody said or thought and just did what she felt was right. It was easy to imagine her at Woodstock being totally free and letting it all hang out.

There were between eight and ten couples there for the training. All of us stared with our mouths hanging open, not saying a word about it, but you could see people making their own decisions about the appropriateness of this incredible sightseeing adventure. Classes were given in her home, which had clean laundry piles all over the place, and in spite of her obviously hectic life she seemed exceedingly organized. She was really quite amazing.

I breast-fed both of my kids for three years, gradually weaning each of them. Sometimes, I thought that they would be seven or eight and going to Christmas dinner at the in-laws and would just come over to me, lift up my shirt, and take a couple of swigs. Fortunately, it never came to that; however, both of them sure hated to give up their nipper napper. Now that they are both grown up, I have no regrets whatsoever because they *both* have beautiful teeth and have had only one cavity each in their entire lives. I, however, have saggy boobs and need lots of dental work.

It's really no wonder that I was constantly riddled with guilt considering my upbringing. I tried to sound cheery and happy and to never let anyone know how unhappy I really was. Like mother, like daughter, we never verbalized our feelings in our family until someone erupted and the shit hit the fan.

When we kids fought, it was nasty—hair pulling, biting, hitting, yelling, and screaming—and our punishments, I realize now, were abusive. Mom did most of the child-rearing since Dad was always out of the house taking care of the farm. Spankings were hard, and she changed into a different person, mean and scary; her face changed into a shrew's, a witch's, a monster's. The rage was just smoldering under the surface like volcanic steam, and we never knew when it would burst out. We were often put into opposite corners of the kitchen and made to kneel facing the wall, sometimes on corncobs and sometimes just on the floor until we could learn to behave ourselves, which was often over an hour.

It didn't matter who was at fault—if you were involved in the dispute, you were punished, and if you cried, she would give you something to cry about: more spanking. We would often have redness, soreness, and bruising on our backsides and legs. If we ever sassed back, we would get our mouths washed out with soap. The more we struggled, the harder she fought to get the soap bar into our mouths. The soap grated against our teeth, and chunks ended up in our mouths. It took a long time to get the soap out of our teeth, and it didn't help one bit to make us behave any better.

All it accomplished was to make us bitter, confused, and angry at each other and at Mom. When Mom was nice, she was very, very nice, but when she was mad, she was horrid.

Our uncle Tommy, Mom's younger brother, made a paddle with some cute saying on it using a woodworking heat tool, and he gave it to Mom as a joke. Ha, ha, fucking ha. She used it often, hitting our legs as we tried to protect ourselves. Adding insult to injury, she had a large pegboard with hooks to hold pots and pans and kitchen utensils and it was right there that she hung that the paddle for all to see. Her anger and frustration at her own life was taken out on her children.

I didn't think I was being abused at the time. It was just the way it was. I thought all kids were punished like this.

I'm sure I married Cheapwad to get as far away as possible, and yet I felt terribly guilty about being so far away and for not calling enough when Mom was diagnosed with MS. Being Catholic, I felt guilty about thinking bad thoughts, masturbating, disobeying my parents, and actually, just about everything.

Lara was born at six pounds five ounces with a very successful childbirth and no anesthesia. At the time, we didn't have a car and relied on public transportation to travel, so one of Cheapwad's friends picked us up at the hospital and took us back to our apartment. I went into our bedroom with the baby, expecting the new daddy to be coming behind us soon. He didn't. He stayed in the kitchen talking to his friend for over three hours before he finally came to see us. By then, I was beyond upset at him and asked him why he elected to be with his friend at a time like this when he should have been with us. His reply was that he felt obligated to his friend because he had taken the time to drive us home. What a guy, huh? I was hurt. I just wanted the three of us to be together and experience our first day as a family. Well, it was the first day of the rest of our days together. He stayed the same, relying on me to raise our daughter and take care of our home while he went out to work and brought home money for us to live and some bacon for me to fry.

Meanwhile, I was finally growing up, changing, seeing myself differently, becoming more alive sexually, and the more I read, the more my mind opened up to new thoughts and ideas. I felt the growing distance between husband number one and me, and as my self-esteem rose, his feelings for me stayed the same—that my only value was that I was always there for him.

Let me just give you one example of how he valued me as a woman; he loved to shop in all of the bargain stores in downtown Manhattan near the AT&T building, and his idea of buying something nice for me was to buy me shirts or pants, mostly men's and slightly irregular sizes and most of which cost a dollar or two. This man was so cheap that once he got a car, he would siphon gas out of wrecked and discarded cars. I told him that we should go out more and have some fun. I said I would like to go bowling sometime, so that Christmas, he got me a bowling game where you had to throw this two-inch-diameter ball at the pins lined up on the rectangular four-foot bowling lane. He was so sure that I was going to absolutely love what he got me for Christmas. I was bowled over all right; I started to laugh hysterically just to hide the tears falling down my face because this was a gift that you would give to an eight-year-old child and certainly not something for a beloved spouse. I'm sure he got a great deal on it from one of the schlock houses he frequented.

He was so cheap that he would steal paper towels and toilet paper from work by putting them in a paper grocery bag, putting the stuff in, and then putting another paper bag inside to cover everything up and then of course putting more stuff in the second bag. We had enough toilet paper and paper towels to last for years and years, not to mention the food trays, the plastic silverware, the typing paper, and whatever else he thought would be useful for us. Talk about bringing home the bacon! He also brought home everything to serve it on.

Being away from my family was tough, but Cheapwad was adamant that we could not afford the airline tickets for me to visit them. Lara was a year and a half old before she ever met my parents or any of her aunts, uncles, and cousins. In the meantime, over the next few years, I began to really want out of the relationship. I felt unappreciated and trapped, yet I could not find a way to do it. I was pretty much isolated, although I had a couple of friends who were also stay-at-home moms. I was feeling more and more that there had to be more to life than this.

It was the time of the women's movement, and the more I read and thought about my life, the more I was ready to explode. Wearing men's clothes that didn't fit me just made me feel dowdy, inappropriate, unsexy, and not at all like I was feeling inside. It had been so ingrained in me to see my worth through Cheapwad's eyes that I was aching for someone to pay attention to me, to value me. By now, I wanted sex a lot more than Cheapwad. It wasn't even just the sex but the communicating and the loving, passionate, embracing feeling that I was missing. Cheapwad's idea of foreplay was about three minutes of groping around the areas he thought were important, such as the clitoris and nipples, completely forgetting about the brain. It was usually over in about fifteen or twenty minutes, and then he would roll over and go to sleep leaving me wanting something more—it wasn't him.

I had never learned how to voice my wants and needs or opinions, and Cheapwad did not want to talk about it. If I did anyway, he thought I was whining and being a baby. It would always end in my outrage and tears and his righteousness. Growing up in my family, it was always the men and boys who had important things to say and were listened to. My two sisters and I learned from Mom to keep our mouths shut and do as we were told, that the man was the boss in the house and the women were there to support their man and stand by their man no matter what; and that the man always had the last say.

Well, I'll tell you, I learned my lesson well. My man wanted me to dress unattractively and to be so shy around other people so I just would not speak up. He molded me to be just what he wanted; he wanted my friends to be gone by the time he got home, dinner on the table, clothes washed and ironed, and his child well cared for by a stay-at-home mom, who was looking so scruffy that no other man would be attracted to her.

But I did change, and I did grow, and I did find myself, so when pre-Fuckwad asked me out to lunch, I was tickled and thrilled beyond belief. I knew it was wrong. I was married with a little girl, and yet I so desperately wanted to be cared for and cared about and to be thought of as attractive and interesting. I wanted to be valued. Bye, bye, Cheapwad. Hello, Fuckwad.

"Thou shalt not lie. Thou shalt not commit adultery . . . Honor thy father and thy mother . . ." I was well on my way to hell!

I remember as a little girl I had lots of urinary tract infections. Doctors' visits were horrible and the humiliation of having to put my legs up in stirrups and cold metal objects inserted inside my vagina was excruciating I didn't know what was wrong with me. I knew I was different from the other kids, and I felt ugly and defective. I had to have a prescription for vaginal suppositories which Mom had to insert in me. Once a day I had to take off my panties, lie down on Mom's bed, and spread my legs, and she would stick one in me. Don't ask me why, but nothing was ever explained to me. It was devastating. I felt bad and nasty. There was never any comforting afterward. I just got up and went on my way.

I had always felt different, and it was a lot of work to hide it. I never talked to anybody about it, and I don't think any of my siblings even knew. But how could they know what was wrong with me? Nobody even told *me* what was wrong with me—not the doctors and not my parents—so I just felt that it was something so bad that it shouldn't even be talked about.

My brother, Ray, had severe hay fever, but he still had to work every summer in the wheat fields, harvesting. He would come home after working all day, his eyes all red and puffy and his face swollen. My parents finally bought him a rubber mask that he had to wear all day in order to keep the air he breathed as clean as possible. It helped some but not enough. I felt so bad for him, and I never understood how Dad could make him do that even though he was so sick. A couple of times, he ended up in the emergency room. And why didn't Mom protect him from that nightmare? He was a farm kid, and he did as he was told. As soon as he graduated from high school, he sped away to Washington State where he still lives and where he is allergic to nothing.

After he left, I took over some of his chores—driving the tractor, baling hay, and hauling it to the haystacks. I remember once driving around and around this pretty steep hill. I was driving the tractor, and Dad was hoisting bales and putting them onto the flatbed trailer. I was always terrified when we got to the really steep parts, afraid that the tractor was going to roll over, but I never voiced my concerns. On one particular day, as I was driving around that hill with the flatbed trailer about three-quarters of the way full, every single one of those bales slid off of the trailer. My dad did not curse very often, but when he did, it was terrifying, and this was one of those times. "God damn it! Shit! Son of a Bitch!" Over and over, he cursed. I don't know how it happened, but Dad had to put all of those bales back on the trailer. It was hard work, and he was already hot and sweaty. I didn't know if he was cursing at me or at the situation, but I felt totally guilty. I felt it was my fault. I felt I had driven the tractor in the wrong way and should have known that those bales would come tumbling down. I was about seventeen at the time, and the work was laborious, the days were long, and I was not meant to be a farmer.

Dad did not say a word about it for the rest of the day or on the way back home; he drove the tractor, and I stood behind him. Back home, we washed up and got ready for dinner, which of course, Mom had ready. During our meal, Dad started to laugh and joke about our foibles of the day, and then I knew it was okay. He never said he was sorry for scaring the hell out of me or cursing like a drunken sailor, but still I knew that deep in his heart, he had let it go and he was sorry. The next morning at dawn, we started doing it all over again, another day as a farmer.

15

BAD CABBIE, BAD, BAD CABBIE

My boss had a Dr. Jekyll—and—Mr. Hyde kind of personality. Everyone at work tiptoed around him and pretty much just kissed his ass. He had some major bipolar issues, and we never knew what to expect. When he was pissed off, you could hear him yelling throughout the whole damn building and everybody would cringe because we knew the rest of the day would not be good.

One day, when I had been out of work from that company for several years (since becoming wheelchair-bound), one of my friends who still worked there knocked unexpectedly at the front door and told Lara that she had some very bad news. Mr. Bipolar had ended up shooting himself in the head in his car while parked in front of his ex-wife's house where his children lived, on the day that their divorce was finalized.

Shortly before that, his company had been taken over by the investors because he was making some very bad and strange executive decisions, so he had lost the company that he had created by really screwing it up, as he had most of his personal relationships. The company was shut down and lots of good people had to look for new jobs. I know that

Mr. Bipolar was a really disturbed man, so I will say nothing more about him except to say that he left two young sons without a daddy and a very big fuck-you to his ex-wife.

I worked at that company for almost ten years, and in the first couple of years, one day out of the blue, Mr. Bipolar came up to me at my desk and offered me two tickets to the Eric Clapton concert playing that night. I was so thrilled because I am a great fan of Eric Clapton and so was my son, who was sixteen years old at the time, so I asked Ryan to come with me. As it turned out, Ryan was sick. He was very disappointed not to be able to go to the concert with me. I was very disappointed that he could not come with me too because I love his company and I wanted to do something fun with him and because my balance while walking had become very precarious and he would have been my guide and protector. My daughter, Lara, was living in Pennsylvania at that time, and I couldn't find anyone else to come with me on such short notice.

I heard two very distinct voices in my head debating whether to go or not to go by myself—to be brave and just do it, or to play it safe and just go on home. One of my voices told me that I really should not go because I was walking so badly and the fatigue was such a major part of getting around, especially so late at night and after a full day of work. To top it all off, I would be going alone and it really wasn't worth the worry and danger that all of that encompassed. That was my reasonable voice, the one who tried to keep me safe and comfortable at all costs.

Now, my other voice, the one who didn't even realize that I had MS or perhaps just didn't give a shit, was urging me to go no matter what and to quit being such a pathetic pussy. Well, I never liked being called a pussy and so I stubbornly decided to go. I called a cab company, asked the guy on the phone about travel arrangements, and told him about my concerns. He assured me that they would get me there and back safely and on time. That calmed me down a little, and I actually started to look forward to going and doing something thrilling and fun. I truly wished I had someone to share this experience with, but what the hell, you only live once, right?

I parked my car outside the gate of my apartment complex, because I did not want the cabdriver to know where I lived. This piece of advice came from my reasonable and thinking-ahead voice.

Anyway, the cabbie showed up and got me to the concert on time and intact. I had a hell of a time inside the arena. I was already tired after a day of work but doggedly, slowly, and dangerously got to my seat, even though there were no handrails to hold on to and no one with me to help me get to my seat. I was already wondering why the hell I had done this to myself. I had to climb down many steps, but I was determined to do this. I was so terribly relieved to finally be able to sit down. There were couples or groups of people all around me, and I felt lonely and alone not having anybody to share this with, talk to, hold hands with, or just to have a shared experience with.

The concert was excellent, and yet, I felt like an old fogey because it was so fucking loud and I was so noise sensitive that I just wanted to die and couldn't wait for the concert to be over. All through the concert, I was wondering how the hell I was going to maneuver my way out of that arena with all those people charging for the doors and me going at a rickety turtle's pace. Well, I did make it out of there; I even stopped to buy my son a concert T-shirt. All the while, I was putting on a smile though I was barely holding myself up with my cane; my arm was literally shaking from the strain of holding myself up as I paid for the shirt and precariously made my way outside.

Once outside, I found the line for cabs, and there were quite a few people on that line. By that time, my legs were so tired I was sure I would fall over any second. And to top it off, there was no sign of my cab—none, nada, nil. I had made arrangements for the cab to be there at a certain time, so I had to call the cab company on my cell phone. A really nice guy answered and said that he would come personally to get me, and he would be there in fifteen or twenty minutes. He said he was so sorry for the mix-up. I think he really meant to say that he was so sorry for the fuck-up, or perhaps he did say that and I just misunderstood.

Meanwhile, I sat down on the curb blessedly thankful to be off my feet and just talked to other people milling around waiting for cabs and chatting about the concert. Some people said they were a little disappointed in Eric's performance, and others thought he was magnificent. I was in the latter group, though I didn't tell them how I really felt about the concert: that my gung-ho voice was an idiot and certainly did not have my best interests at heart. I vowed then and there never to listen to that voice again; for God's sake, what was I thinking? To tell you the truth, the only reason I went was to prove to myself that I could do it. Well, I did. Goody for me! Yahoo! I couldn't wait to get to bed, because I had to go to work the next day and pretend I had a great time. I knew that I was going to have to kiss my boss's big hairy ass, which was expected of everyone who wanted to work there—not that any of us really wanted to work there, but it was so damn scary to look for another job that we all just kind of stayed and complained among ourselves.

Lord have mercy, my taxi van finally appeared. The cabdriver said that the back doors were not working, so I would have to sit in the front seat. He helped me into the front passenger seat because it was a van and I had trouble getting into those what with the MS and all. Bells were already starting to go off in my head. This just did not seem right, but I was so exhausted that I just wanted to get home. As I got into the front seat, I was thinking to myself that I should have had him prove to me that the back doors did not work. A day late and a dollar short, as the saying goes. Where was my rational thinking voice when I needed it?

As we were traveling, he asked me a lot of personal questions. Did I live alone? I lied and told him my husband and sons were home waiting for me. He asked about where I was from and why I had to use a cane, and then he started to stroke my hair and my face. Now the bells were turning into sirens. I was becoming very uncomfortable and frightened. He was telling me how beautiful I was and how much he loved my hair. Holy shit! I told him not to do that to me, and he stopped for a while. He said he did not mean to offend me in his Middle-Eastern-accented voice. (I don't really care what country you come from or what you look like, just do your fucking job professionally and without any added benefits.) He started to touch my hair again, and again, I told him to stop it, that I was happily married and

I did not like what he was doing. And still he was talking about how sweet I was and saying that he liked me very much. It seemed like a really long ride home, and I thought perhaps he was taking a circuitous route to make the ride a little longer. I was in the front seat of a van with a total stranger; I was exhausted and disabled and not able to just open the door and jump out, which would have been sure death since we were on the freeway anyway, so I was stuck there with this fucking freak.

Finally, we made it home, and thankfully, I had parked outside of the gate. I paid him, even giving him a tip, fearing that it would upset him in some way if I didn't and put me in further danger. As I was getting out of the van, he asked me if he could help me. I told him I was fine, while I struggled to get myself down the tall steps of the van, and as I was starting to walk-hobble to my car, he followed me and asked if I needed any help getting into my car. Unfortunately at the time, I did not have Life Alert to be able to just press a button around my neck and have someone come and rescue me. I told him, "No, I am okay. I don't need any help." Still following me, he handed me a business card with his name and telephone number written on the back and said if I ever needed a ride again that I could call him directly. I said, "Thank you" and "Good night." I unlocked my car door, got in, and locked the door as soon as I could, and in my rearview mirror, I finally saw him drive away. I was thankful he did not follow me through the gate.

The next day at work, I called the taxi company and made a formal complaint about the fucker who happened to be from some terrorist refugee country, but the guy on the phone said that they had no one there by the name that was written on the back of the card and he was sure that none of his people would do any of the things that I had accused his driver of doing because they were so thoroughly trained in the proper policies and procedures when dealing with the public. I was so mad I could have spit and I was yelling into the phone. People were coming to the door of the reception room to see what the problem was. I got no satisfaction at all from talking to this schmuck, so I finally slammed the phone down. I explained to the gathering crowd what had happened, and they were all properly horrified.

Next, I called the taxi commission and told one of the agents the whole story. The commissioner took everything very seriously. The agent said that taxi company owners almost always took the side of the drivers, so I should not get my hopes up, but he would be in touch and would investigate thoroughly. He asked a couple more questions to get more details, but nothing ever came of the case. Shit! Shit! Shitty, shit, shit!

I hope to discover that this illegal alien terrorist fuck face ate some rotten falafel, suffered horribly, and had to have his stomach pumped. I hope the suction thingy accidentally sucked up part of his stomach lining causing massive internal hemorrhaging, which then caused him to be hospitalized, where they found out that he was here in the United States illegally and he was sent back to his mother freakin' country in great pain and is now a castaway because he deserted his fellow countrymen and went to the land of many infidels. I hope the local doctors use fresh, right-out-of-the-camel dung to treat his wounds and he is forced to beg for food in the stench-filled streets.

That'll teach him not to mess with vulnerable women of any nationality, especially those who are disabled and are walking with canes. All I wanted was a no-touching, no-sweet-talking, backseat taxi ride to my home.

Bad Cabbie! Bad! Bad! Motherfucking Cabbie!

16

Don't Bother
the Crippled Lady

Ah, the wonder of childhood. Children are so curious, so inquisitive, so wonderingly investigative and so eager to learn about their world. Most kids who are sitting in the passenger rack of a shopping cart are at just about the same height as I am in my wheelchair, so when we pass each other in the aisles, I will smile at them and say hi. Almost all of them will smile and say hi to me in return. Often, I will wave at them, and they will wave as well, as their parents or caregivers go blindly on oblivious to our little interaction. Sometimes, the parents will say something like, "Say hi to the nice lady, Connie, Priscilla, Johnny, or Junior," or whatever the kid's name happens to be.

I really love and appreciate when kids approach me just wanting to know what the heck is going on here. Once in a while, a kid will ask what's wrong with me, and before the little guy can even finish his sentence, his mother will whisk him away, saying something ridiculous like "Don't be rude," or "Don't bother the nice lady," or just whisk him around so his body is turned away from me. His head is usually still turned toward me, and he is still making eye contact. What I would really like to do is tell the mother that *she* should not be so rude because it disrespects me and her little person. I mean, for heaven's sake, the only thing she's teaching her kid is to avoid handicapped people and to never ever, under any circumstances, interact with them. What the fuck does she think is going to happen? Does she think her kid's gonna catch something like wheelchairitis, or left-side-of-the-body paralysis, or maybe even, God forbid, a willingness to learn something new—or even worse than that, empathy?

One little kid, he must've been about four or five years old, asked me what had happened to me. Though his mother tried to get him away from me as quickly and as far away as possible, he managed to break free from her Wrestle Mania-type grip and turn back to me with curiosity spread all over his face like peanut butter on bread. I gave him a big smile and told him that my legs didn't work very well. He replied, "Your legs don't work so good?" I answered him, "No, they don't."

He just said, "Oh," turned around, and went back to his mom—reluctantly, I am sure, because she had four kids with her and looked like she had just taken her steroids for the day and really just wanted to be left the fuck alone. That kid is going to end up being either a news anchor or spending most of his time in solitary confinement in the big house, as will his mother. All he needed from me was acknowledgment and proof that someone would listen to him and help him get his curiosity satisfied.

Since I travel with the Handi-ride bus built especially for wheelchairs with that wonderful ramp that lifts the chair up and down hydraulically, I get a lot of attention from the wee ones when I am being transported. All the kids are interested in this contraption since they've probably never seen anything like it before and they are just aching to take a ride for themselves. Some of the adults with them will watch with them, curious themselves or at least patient with their children, and then again, there is the other group of whiskers-away. I don't suppose it would be proper protocol to yell at them as I am slowly going down to the ground. "Hey, wait! Look at this! Look what I can do! Isn't this great?"

One day, when I was scooting around Walgreens, I had to try to reach something that was on the very top shelf that I couldn't get to even with my reacher. A woman and her little girl, who was probably about age ten, happened to come around the corner. I asked the woman if she would help me get what I needed. "Of course, what do you need?" the mom replied.

The girl said in a very excited voice, "I'll get it for you!" So the two acted as a team: the mom got the things from the top shelf, and the girl brought them to me. It was frozen pizza, on sale two for five dollars. I had coupons saying, "Buy one, get one free," so they were a little over a dollar each, and nothing makes me happier than being able to use great coupons on great sale items. And the girl, whose name I had by then learned was Michelle, kept up a conversation, telling me that her grandma was in a wheelchair and she helped her all the time. She asked me why I was in a wheelchair, and I told her I had a disease called MS and I was not able to walk but I was still able to get around and do what I needed to do. Michelle didn't blink an eye and went on to tell me that her dog Mimi had arthritis and didn't walk very well either. Her mother, meanwhile, was just standing a few steps behind beaming at her wonderful child, and believe me, that child was wonderful—not an ounce of discomfort or shyness and a ton of perky generosity and caring. Her mother had done a damned good job of raising her. Still yakking away a mile a minute, Michelle asked if there was anything else that I needed that she could help me with, so I spotted something on a lower shelf—Oscar Mayer hot dogs—and asked her if she could give me two of those, which she did with pure delight. I didn't really want them since I hadn't eaten red meat in at least thirty-five years. I later put them back, but it was well worth it just to see this little angel in action. I thanked her profusely and asked if I could have a hug, and she gave me a good, long squeeze, which I returned with my one good hand. As we were saying good-bye, she said if there was anything else that I needed, I should just yell for her and she would rush over to help me.

Michelle is an old soul, and she will end up doing great works in this world, perhaps as someone the caliber of Mother Teresa or a talk show host taking over when Oprah leaves her throne; Michelle will grow up to be someone so special that no one could fill her shoes.

Anyway, Michelle, you are a shining light, as is your mother, who could teach a lot of people how doing such a small thing for someone else can leave such a long and lasting impression. May the force be with both of you.

17

Dear God, Please Don't Let Me Pee On *Oprah!*
(The TV Show, Not the Gal)

Exacerbate. There's a word for ya. It is what stress will do to this ugly mess of a disease. Stress will exacerbate MS symptoms. This is not the same as *masturbate*, which is actually good for MS as well as anyone else dealing with stress. But here again, I digress.

My confidence and self-image have so radically changed since I have started seeing Dr. Cinzia over a year ago that I am now actually writing a book about the adventures I have had with this dastardly, debilitating disease. Dr. Cinzia relentlessly and repeatedly asks me to think about what I have learned along the way. There have been times when I really have not wanted to go to the appointments with her because enough is enough already. Then again, enough is not enough already, because I gain insights every time I go, and amazingly, the things that we have talked about in therapy materialize in one way or another within days of my session. I am learning more and more to pay attention to the clues that the universe puts right in front of my nose. Postponing looking at those clues and hints will just delay my progress and tiny little bells will turn into hammers on the head until I finally learn the lesson and learn it well. It is so much easier and more fulfilling and it leads to a much happier and more satisfying life if you just fucking pay attention and fucking learn from the start.

When I want to go someplace, I must first make arrangements with the Handi-ride bus. You need to make appointments at least a day in advance. The bus usually comes, usually on time and miraculously takes you from door to door and back again. The day I finally broke down and applied for a Handi-ride card was a day that my independence grew in leaps and bounds. I no longer have to rely on anyone else to get to my doctors' offices or the symphony or a restaurant or Walgreens or anywhere my trusty motorized wheelchair and I want to go. Oh goodness, here I go again, off on a tangent in a direction I didn't mean to go.

Oh yeah, I was talking about stress and the need to avoid it. First of all, let me just say that it is so ridiculous to say we should avoid stress. Any doctor who says it from now on should be tarred and feathered—then we'll see how well he or she can avoid stress. Anyway, I have been writing something for every session I go to, whether it about Fuckwad or dealing with the motherfucking incontinence, depression, or losing control of my body and my ability to move, so yes, it is stressful and yes, dear Dr. Cinzia, I have learned much along the way.

Well, now, the thing is Dr. Cinzia had been urging me for at least the last six sessions to work really hard at compiling my writings and get them into book form so that it will be ready well before Oprah leaves her show. She believes that what I have to say and the way in which I say it would be very inspirational and unlike anything that has been written about disability. I imagine she means no one curses as much as I do in this sort of book. I had not thought about it that way before, but as I've grown and opened myself up to new possibilities, I've become very excited to think that I may actually have a way to help more people than I ever have before. She asked me when I think I will be ready, and even though I'm not really sure, I told her probably in about two months.

Now my darling Dr. Cinzia has a PhD in clinical psychology, and sure as shootin', you gotta know that the thought of being on Oprah's schedule caused me more than a little stress. Wouldn't you think that Dr. Cinzia, with all her knowledge and experience, would just leave me the fuck alone already? It is amazing to think that my story would be perfect for a venue like *Oprah* and could possibly open up conversation. Are you sure Dr. Cinzia? Because the stress is killing me here.

So now I am thinking of all the things that I have to do, besides finishing the book, in order to get ready to go on the *Oprah* show. I'm thinking really big here to make my dreams come true.

First concern, I have to take all the precautions not to have to pee on *Oprah*. Second of all, what will I wear? And then I'm sure we will have to do it by satellite or Skype because traveling by plane is always stressful. And having MS, I have to deal with the goddamn fatigue, and, God what if they have to strip search me and put me in a line with potential terrorists?

Then of course, I will be unbelievably star struck to be actually chatting with my heroine, known the world over by just one name: Oprah! I'm sure there will be people there to do my hair and makeup and won't that be lovely. It would be just so groovy if we could do the interview from Dr. Cinzia's office where all the action takes place anyway, and Dr. Cinzia could fill in for me when I am speechless or my mouth is stuck shut from all the damn meds I have to take. I realize it's a little early to start fretting because I've still got quite a bit more work to do on the book, but I would so much love to be taken under Oprah's wings. But then, wouldn't we all?

Now that is clearly not going to happen since I wrote the above and our dear Oprah has gone on to other things and left us in the lurch I will have to think of someone else's wings to glide beneath. Maybe Dr Phil or Jimmy Kimmel. I would love to share my message of growth and blessing no matter what your circumstances are in life and to be able to do it with a fucking great sense of humor and the help, wisdom, and strength of Dr. Cinzia right there at my side.

I do want to give a different voice to people with disabilities and to show that there is strength, resilience, adaptability, and most of all, a sense of humor about the disease, major malfunction, disability, depression, or whatever the hell is wrong with you because there are burdens to bear and lessons to be learned for every single one of us, even the healthiest of nuts and the strongest of men. The greatest gift that Dr. Cinzia has given me is her strong belief in me and in the messages that I have written along the way. She has urged me to share the lessons of my journey, which has been so hard, so terrifying, and so humiliating. At the same time,

I have been shedding layer upon layer of all that shit that I'd pummeled, starting from a very early age, deep into my very being. Why should it be any surprise that I started to feel such *dis*-ease and that it manifested itself by creating the debilitating, incurable disease I've come to know so well: MS, also known as motherfucking shitwad disease?

I have come to accept and embrace the idea that Oprah and Phil and Jimmy would recognize the truth and validity of my various essays. They're all to be put together to create a book that chronicles my own personal spiritual journey, and yes, I am very spiritual, despite all of the goddamned cursing that happens to spurt out of my potty mouth, into the Dragon voice recognition program, and onto the page every now and then. I have been visualizing my book in a reader's hands and in the front window of Borders (Holy crap! No more Borders! How the hell did they let e-books slip from their corporate little mitts?) as well as Barnes & Noble and on Amazon's website. I don't want to offend any of the big guys in the bookselling trade by leaving out their names.

Which reminds me, what the hell is happening to our school system and our nation in general when libraries are being closed because of budget cuts? What does that say not only to our children, who rely on libraries to do research and study for school and take out as many books as their book bags will hold and also to those who want to learn and who retain a love of reading? And what kind of message does this convey to just anyone who uses the library, who can't afford books or computers or magazines or newspapers?

And here is a shout-out to every librarian in every library in the world, because they really are the gatekeepers and the heroes of one of the greatest assets of civilization. Poor Benjamin Franklin must be rolling over in his grave just thinking about what is happening to his beloved library system. It breaks my heart too, Ben, and when I die, I will be rolling over as well, but it will be in an urn because I will be cremated. I think that those budget cuts should come out of some of the horrible waste in our government or perhaps a small percentage of the pay given to tobacco and insurance company lobbyists. That would surely pay for enough libraries to be convenient to every citizen in the United States. And the lobbyists will still be living high off the hog.

Sorry about the tangent above, but it had to be said. I love libraries.

18

The Wheels on the Bus Go Round and Round

Signing up for the Handi-ride bus service was just about the best thing I've ever done. I was very skeptical about using this service, and I had heard some horror stories and negative things said about it. I'm not the kind of person who just jumps into things; I have to mull it over and think about it and let it swirl around in my brain for quite a while before I finally take the plunge. In the case of the bus service, it took me at least three years to finally take that first step, and I only did that because it was becoming increasingly difficult and dangerous for Brian or Lara to transport me in the car.

It got to the point where we would end up in tears with the struggle of getting me into the car and several times had to call Life Alert to come and rescue me and that is just about the best thing I've done as a disabled person. Just the press of a button hanging on a string around my neck and Life Alert is there within 10 or 15 minutes and I am rescued once again from another fine mess I've gotten myself into. There really have been times when I have fallen and not been able to get up.

Anyone out there who is alone during the day and could put him—or herself in danger should sign up for this wonderful service immediately. It is phenomenal, and not only that, but five or six gorgeous fireman will show up, lift you up as though you were a rag doll, and put you back where you belong. I've come to know them pretty well by now, and they have seen me in all sorts of contortions and predicaments, sometimes in the shower totally naked. Under normal circumstances, I would not mind one little bit being naked and being picked up by a big, strong man, but that is not the case in these situations.

I did tell them on one particular call for help that the next time they showed up, I wanted them to be naked and I would have some clothes on—it only seemed fair. They got a good chuckle out of it, but the next time they had to show up, they were still in uniform. You know who you are, all my heroes at Fire Station Number 3 in Carrollton, Texas. Oh well, what can you do? You can get a fireman to respond to an emergency, but you can't make him show up naked.

Anyway, back to the bus service. It seems that one of the negative side effects of being a driver for the Handi-ride buses is a proclivity to put on a great deal of weight since they don't really get breaks and have to eat on the run, which means fast food. They also don't really drink enough—water, that is; they don't want to have to stop and go to the bathroom very often. Most of the drivers are really nice, caring, and helpful. But once in a while, you get one who is not a people person and would really do much better working as a guard in the prison system or perhaps as one of those people who collects snake venom for antidotes.

I had one bus driver, bless his heart, who was so obese he didn't even climb down the four steps out of the bus to maneuver the wheelchair ramp; he just stood up with great difficulty and maneuvered the machinery from inside the bus, which I believe is not correct protocol. Since this was in summertime in Texas, just the act of getting out of his chair had him sweating so profusely it was as though there was a sprinkler above his head and droplets were just plopping down, soaking his clothing.

Next, he had to attach the safety chains to my wheelchair, and to do so, he had to reach down and all the way across me to attach the left side front chain. I had to turn off my electric wheelchair because he kept bumping the control panel with his gigantic belly and moving my chair in different directions.

Finally, all four chains were secured, and my seat belt held me safely in place. He huffed and puffed the two feet back to his chair. I felt so sorry for him. He had not the energy to utter even one word, and I was so afraid that he was going to have a heart attack somewhere along the way to our destination and I was going to have to drive him to the emergency room. Aye, yai, yai! I really meant it when I said, "Bless his heart," because his heart is going to need all the prayers it can get.

One time, when I was coming back from seeing Dr. Cinzia, I had a female driver who was very friendly, even a little too chatty. I just wanted to get home in peace and quiet and she informed me that she could really go for a bowl of chili. She was really hungry and really in the mood for a nice hot bowl of chili. I had no answer to that, thinking she was just making idle talk. Suddenly, she turned into a fast-food restaurant and parked the bus, which was nothing unusual; I was thinking that we were there to pick up another passenger. It happens all the time.

All of a sudden, she jumped up out of her seat and said to me, "You don't mind if I just run in and get a bowl of chili, do you?" She had already opened the bus door and was halfway down the steps when she asked me, "Do you want one?" Now believe me I knew this was totally against the rules. I told her, "No, nothing for me," and let her be on her way.

They must've been very busy in the restaurant, because it sure took her a goddamn long time. I was getting a little agitated because we only had about ten minutes left before I was home. Why she couldn't wait until after she dropped me off to get her goddamn food, I don't know. But I guess it was the nearest place that had chili, it was chili that she needed, and nobody was gonna stop her. I didn't say anything to her. I just let it go, because it certainly wasn't worth making a fuss over. I knew that if I did put in a complaint, she would surely get a talking to, and I really didn't want her to get in trouble. At any rate, I finally got home safe and sound. And then she could eat her chili.

There is a big sign by the front window of the buses that states in very large letters that everyone must wear a seat belt. That certainly makes sense, since anybody can get into an accident at any time and not everyone is courteous to handicapped people or to the buses they ride in. The most impatient ones, of course, drive convertible sports cars. There are many people who don't want to let handicapped people get in front of them. These people just don't deserve the privilege of having a driver's license. You'd be amazed at how many times the Handi-ride buses get cut off or are put in dangerous situations on our public highways and byways.

Anyway, the bus driver I had on this particular ride had locked only three of the chains onto my wheelchair, and I told him that he forgot one. He said, "Oh, you're right. I forgot about that one," and he hooked it up.

And then—get a load of this—he asked me if I wanted my seat belt on! What are you, a *fucking idiot*? Did you think I would say, "No, that's okay. You look like a great driver, and I'm sure I'll be perfectly safe. No need for you to have to go through the trouble of putting a seat belt around me. I trust you." But what I really wanted to do was slap him across his goofy-looking face and ask him if his mother was still one of the exhibits at the Dallas petting zoo. But no, not me, Ms. Nice Guy. I told him, "Of course, put my seatbelt on." What a wanker. I guess it takes all kinds, but common sense should prevail, especially when you have someone else's safety in your hands. But like they say, common sense is not all that common.

I guess bus drivers are just like anybody else—a little of this and a little of that; some are frickin' smart, and some are just too frickin' stupid to bother with because they don't have a chance in hell of changing. So far, I have only reported the drivers I have really liked and who do an excellent job and really are people persons.

We as riders of the city bus system are urged to call or write in complaints about inappropriate behavior or unsafe drivers. I'll tell you the truth though, by the time I get home I am usually so exhausted I just want to lie down and forget all about the stupid bus driver and his obese belly and never actually report anyone even though I have every intention of doing it later. Ha! Never happens.

I'm sure there will come a day when I will report someone who should actually have no contact with other human beings whatsoever. It's come close, but I've given them a break because I realize that I have done some of the most stupid-ass things you could ever imagine while I was still able to drive which was about six years ago. And so in the course of life, it's just a piss in the wind; hopefully, the wind will be with me.

19

DR. CINZIA SUCKS THE BIG ONE

And here's why: first of all, let me just say that I adore Dr. Cinzia and her arrival has been a miracle in my life, and yet . . . she just won't leave me the fuck alone. "We are not done with Fuckwad," she says. "Think about him. Write about him. Jot down your random thoughts of him. We need to get to the bottom of your betrayal and pain and your pattern of putting yourself in vulnerable situations with men, and especially Fuckwad." Fuckwad this, Fuckwad that, and Fuckwad the other. I just want to forget about that devious bastard and not to be obligated to dredge up painful incidences that I can't bear to relive. But *no*, not with fucking Dr. Cinzia. "You are doing great work, Renae," she says. "You are stronger and wiser, and no man will ever treat you the way Fuckwad did again."

Well, that's for damn sure. I'll give you that much, Dr. Cinzia. Thanks to you, I've got Fuckwad on my mind yet again.

Then tonight, when I sat down to write about Fuckwad, something strange happened. I drew a blank. I couldn't think of any more cruel or mean things he said or did to me. Huh, what do you know about that?

124

Unless of course you count the numerous times he called me nothing but a cunt, a bloodsucking leech of a cunt. Or the time when I went to my mom's funeral in North Dakota, as I described earlier, and he demanded I come home early. I relied on him for help and support, but after I had been there for only four days, Fuckwad called me, not to find out how I was doing or how everybody else was doing, but to tell me to come back because he couldn't do it all himself and he needed me there to help with Ryan and the store.

So I had to tell my family that I had to leave the next day because I was needed at the store and the business was more important than time spent with my family after our mother and Dad's wife of fifty years had died. Of course, I didn't really tell my family that, but that's exactly what I was thinking; I wasn't ready to leave yet, but nonetheless, Lara and I packed up and left the next morning.

When we got to the airport, Lara took a cab back to the apartment she shared with her boyfriend and I took a cab from Newark Airport to our store. I peed in my pants in the cab. I just couldn't hold it in, and at the time, I knew nothing about catheters or any incontinence supplies. It was the beginning of a new chapter in my life's saga with MS. So anyway, I paid the poor guy. I was sure he would be flabbergasted when he found out that his last fare had soaked the backseat of his cab with urine or, God forbid, another person got into the cab and sat in the pee that I had left behind as a little surprise. Now I am formally apologizing to that cabdriver and any patrons who happened to sit in a puddle of pee; it was yet another totally humiliating incident traveling with such a fucked-up disease.

When I walked into the store with soaking-wet clothes, I said a quick hello, and as fast as my decrepit little body would go, I went upstairs to change and then went to give a huge hug and kisses to my little boy and to Fuckwad, who at the time was still somewhat acting like my loving husband and partner and not the Fuckwad I would later come to fear and have terrifying nightmares about. He was just so happy to see me there for him once again—just the way it was supposed to be.

Not once in all the years we've been divorced—twelve years already and I'm still talking about him in therapy—has he ever sent a card or a gift for Lara's birthday or for Christmas; nor has he called just to see how she is doing. He raised her from the age of six, and he was her father figure, so he basically deserted her as well. One time, Fuckwad's new wife sent a gift certificate to Lara and signed it from both of them, but I truly doubt that he ever even knew about it.

Just as tragic is that in all the years we've been divorced, Fuckwad has never apologized or for that matter said, "I am sorry," in any way, shape, or form for all that he put me through. I don't think he ever thinks about it or has any notion of how deeply I was affected. I think that once he got his way and found a new life with the help and support of his new woman, he just totally forgot about the past and has no idea of the gut-wrenching fear that I had to overcome in order for our son to have a mom and dad, because I knew that Fuckwad was going to move to Dallas no matter what and I knew that MS was taking its toll on me and that I wouldn't be able to take care of Ryan the way he needed to be taken care of on my own. And Fuckwad was.

So really and truly, Dr. Cinzia doesn't suck the big one, unless she is lucky enough in her personal life to do so. To keep to the boundaries between doctor and patient, I am not allowed to ask her any such personal questions, although I am dying to know. And right now, I love and appreciate every horrible thought she's gotten me to face. The memories are getting fuzzier and fuzzier, and my dreams and nightmares have changed as the lessons are learned and new ones come along. My life is busy, so I don't have a lot of time to think about that motherfucking Fuckwad and all of his evil doings.

The peace that I feel to be free of that torment is tremendous. I look back on it now, and I'm really quite astonished that I was able to do what I did. I transferred my whole life from New York City to Dallas, Texas, and built something out of nothing. I had no money, no job, no car, no telephone or TV service of any kind, and very little self-esteem. I gave my life up to the universal powers and literally took one day at a time, one task at a time. The closest pay phone was probably a quarter-mile away, and I had to make that trek over and over again with my trusty cane and hanging onto the side rails; I would be thoroughly exhausted by the time I reached the pay phone to get my services connected—for the phone which took five days. I was lonely and depressed, and way back then, I did not have a cell phone. I felt cut off from the world.

Slowly but surely, things started to come together, and I built a life out of the ether and stone-cold determination in order to have my children see me as strong and accomplished, even though I felt weak, fatigued, lost, and betrayed. I smiled and put on a jolly good show for my son and daughter and even for Fuckwad because I did not want him to see me fall completely to pieces.

Every now and then, a memory will surface, but I don't cry about it anymore, and the Fuckwad-induced pain is dissipating as new patterns reach my consciousness.

Dr. Cinzia, I am sorry about the whole beginning of this piece, but what other therapist would appreciate the love and gratitude behind the words?

20

OCD—Obsessive-Compulsive Disorder

(Not Her Real Name)

This is the impairment that my second health care aide suffers from—no doubt about it—and she passed every bit of that suffering on to me. The first thing she wanted to do was to sit down together and figure out what our schedule was going to be. She wanted to know exactly which days I would want to have a shower, which days she was to take out the trash, which day to do the laundry, etc. She made it clear to me that having rules was the way that she worked best.

I told her that I didn't work on a strict schedule, because every day was different for me, but we would settle into a routine and do the best we could. OCD didn't seem all that pleased but said that we would do the best we could to work together. Those last two words were not lost on me. We were not here to work together. She was here to work for me. I really need to learn to be a hard-ass but being a wimpy pussy comes so much more naturally to me.

So she decided that my showers were to be taken on Tuesdays and Fridays so that when I said very early on that I wanted to take a shower, she made it known that it was only a Monday. Even though I wanted to cut off her fat little fingers and feed them to my dog, I restrained myself from doing her any bodily harm and told her it didn't matter which day it was, I needed to take a shower.

Now I've said it before and I'm going to say it again here: I don't care what color you are, what size you are, what religion you are, or anything about you as long as you have a good heart and are doing your goddamned fucking job. Well, being good at your job as a home health aide means being strong enough to help the people who you were hired to help to get into and out of the shower or on and off the toilet or the bed or wherever they need to get to. At least that was my understanding until OCD let it be known that the aides didn't get any health insurance and they were only supposed to do what they thought they could do safely in order not to get hurt themselves.

And apparently, as I was to learn in short order, in OCD's case, that meant being of very little help getting into and out of the shower because she was not strong enough to lift me. Instead, she just stood very, very close to me with her hand on my shoulder making me very uncomfortable. She also didn't take instruction very well and had her own way of doing things. I felt that I was really in danger with this hovering hulk of unhelpful OCD unprofessionalism. She made me so nervous, I just wanted to punch her in the stomach, since I couldn't reach her face, and I would have too if it weren't for the fact that I was naked and in a vulnerable position and quite afraid of her retaliation.

It was very hard for me and exhausting just to get from my wheelchair onto my sliding shower chair. She washed my hair and my body, and somehow, I got back onto the wheelchair. From then on, while OCD was my aide, we did my bathing at the kitchen sink, which was an ordeal in itself, but at least it was safer than the shower.

One of the tasks that I asked her to help me with was cutting out coupons from the Sunday newspaper inserts. OCD was not so happy about this, but since it was in her job description to assist me in a hobby or other task, she had no choice. I showed her how to do it, and since I had four or five of the same inserts, I showed her how to stack them one upon the other and cut them all at the same time, which I figured would save her a lot of time and hardship since her heart was not in it. Tough shit, OCD, just shut up and do what I fucking asked you to do without your goddamn attitude.

She, however, had ideas of her own. She insisted on doing only two pages at a time and was exceptionally meticulous, but the thing that made me want to slap her silly was that she would take all of the paper that was garbage and one sheet at a time after the coupons were cut, would fold them into tinier and tinier pieces. I'm serious. She needed to fold every single piece of garbage newspaper. I told her that she did not need to do that and all she had to do was just throw it in the recycling box I had put right beside her. She gave me a look as though I had just purposefully farted in her face and told me in a very stern voice that this was the way that she liked to do it. OCD had some hostility issues as well. Now mind you, she'd only been there for about three weeks, and I figured I should give it a little more time. Maybe she would simmer down.

I have been told by every aide that I have come across that they really like to work for me because I am very easygoing and sweet. As I continue to go to therapy every week, I am learning that being sweet and nice to people doesn't mean that I have to allow them to take advantage of me and make me uncomfortable in my own home when it is their job to take care of me and make sure that I am comfortable and have more time to do the things that will bring joy to my life.

So one morning, OCD was doing her usual things—doing the dishes, cleaning the floors, yada, yada, yada—and I was working at my computer on some insurance issues. I had hit the doughnut hole, which if you don't know what that is, it is when you have reached the limit of what your insurance will pay and what you are responsible for the rest of the year. For me, that meant Social Security disability and a secondary United Healthcare Insurance, and I still had six months in which I had to pay 100 percent of all my pharmaceutical drugs, which added up to a lot of money. So there I was in a dither.

I figured I would be better able to handle it if I ate something first, so I asked OCD politely to make me two pieces of toast with peanut butter. Not too hard to do, right? Well, if you answered yes, you would be wrong, because apparently, even though she helped me get my breakfast every other day, today, she was going to take a stand. She was standing over by the stove about five feet away from me and said to me in a very firm tone, "Ms. Renae." I was a little startled so I turned around to look at her, and there she was, arms akimbo. She looked like the teapot in that song that goes:

> I'm a little teapot short and stout;
> Here is my handle, here is my spout.
> When I get all steamed up, then I shout,
> Just tip me over and pour me out.

I found out from Wikipedia, that this little ditty was originally written by George Harold Sanders and Clarence Z. Kelley and published in 1939 and was featured as a haunted rhyme that the villain psychically transmits throughout Stephen King's "Storm of The Century" TV movie in 1999. The song is also sung in another Stephen King movie "Rose Red" by the ghost of the child character April Rimbauer. Thank you Steven King for ruining that cute little song forever!! Yikes!

OCD went on to say, "You are sitting over there at your computer, and my job is to help you to do things that you cannot do for yourself. I know you can put bread in the toaster and put on your own peanut butter!"

What the fuck? Where the hell did that come from? Did she really need me to explain to her what I was doing, why I was doing it, and why I asked her to do something for me? Meanwhile, she had come very close to me, still in her little teapot pose, and even though she was only about five two, she was very round and was still hovering over me. She was really giving me the creeps. Apparently, I had overstepped the bounds that her OCD ass could handle. Here, yet again, I was being intimidated and harassed by a home health aide. Apparently, I still had lots to learn about setting the boundaries for how I would let people treat me.

I told her I was really upset and couldn't talk about it right then, and I sent her home. Since this happened on a Friday, I had the weekend to figure out how I was going to handle it and what I was going to say.

When she showed up Monday, I was actually going to speak to her at the end of her shift with me, but she said she first wanted to talk to me about something. "Sit down," I told her, "because I have something to say to you first. You have been speaking to me very rudely, and you get very huffy and treat me with disrespect. I won't have that in my own home, and for those reasons, I don't want you to come back." Without saying a word, she gathered her things and left. I had wanted her to make my bed, clean the floors, and do a couple of other chores first before I fired her sorry teapot ass, but what the hell? She was gone, and I was so relieved—relieved and also proud of myself that I had handled it relatively gracefully and yet forcefully.

The only thing now was that I was going to have to train a brand-new aide. Son of a goddamn bitch, it never fucking ends.

21

NO HABLA INGLÉS

So now I am on my third aide with Blessings Home Healthcare Agency. Nofi, my beautiful Nigerian aide, who has only been with me for about a month and who has been just wonderful, has gone to Africa to visit her family in Nigeria for at least six weeks, which means training another brand-new aide, yet again. Fuckity, fuckity, fuck, fuck, fuck!

One day, out of the blue, the director of the agency, let's just call her Grog, showed up at my door unexpectedly with a woman I had never seen before. She introduced this woman to me as Sandra and said she would be my new aide. I was really surprised that they showed up at the door without calling first and letting me know that they were coming. I shook Sandra's hand, said hello, and invited them to come in. Connie, oh, I meant Grog, the director, started speaking. Sandra just stood there like a deer in the headlights.

The whole thing seemed rather peculiar to me. Then Grog told me that Sandra spoke very little English, and I understood why they did not call before they came. I would have said, "*No*, absolutely not!" I knew I could not have a non-English-speaking aide, but since they were already

135

there, how could I say no and not insult Sandra at the same time? So I said that we would give it a try until Nofi came back from Africa and see how it went. I did not realize it at the time, but I figured it out later, Nofi had to go back to Africa to renew her visa. No one at the agency had given me the courtesy of notifying me that this would happen. Bad agency, bad, bad agency!

Meanwhile, I was going to have to train another aide to do things the way I wanted them to be done. I didn't speak Spanish, and Sandra did not speak very much English. In my mind, I was thinking, *What the fuck? How dare they do that to a person who needs help! This is totally crazy! They are talking out of their minds!* And now I'm thinking that they finagled me into this because they had no one else available. Had I known this from the beginning, I would definitely have gone to a different agency. But I figured I would give it a try until Nofi came back. Besides, how bad could it really be?

I explained to Sandra what I needed to have done—general housekeeping; laundry; cleaning my catheter supplies; helping me to shower; sweeping, vacuuming, and mopping the floors; and helping me with my coupon cutting. Just getting her to understand how I needed my bed to be made so that I could transfer from my wheelchair into the bed was a chore, and for five days in a row, I had to show her over and over again—which meant me actually doing it the way I wanted it to be done while she pretended to understand, smiled, nodded, and said, "Yes, I know, I know."

No, you don't, you big booger. You don't have the faintest clue what I've just said.

On the third day, I called Grog the supervisor back, really upset that they had sent me a non-English-speaking aide. I told her that Sandra did not understand me when I told her what to do; she pretended to understand but did it the wrong way. And I was also just very upset by the fact that they had showed up at my door without even calling. I felt it was very unprofessional.

I knew there was a comeback coming, so I wasn't surprised when Grog said she had tried to call but there was no answer. Bullshit, Grog, bullshit! I didn't actually say it, but I knew it. I continued on with my complaints: when Sandra was supposed to help me get into the shower, I felt my life was in danger because she had no idea what she was doing and had certainly had no training on how to do it. It was such a vital thing for an aide to know how to do.

In addition, she finished clipping the coupons so quickly I knew it wasn't possible for it to be right. I checked it when she was gone that day and found that half of the coupons had been thrown in the trash and some whole sections of the newspaper inserts were just trashed. Grog started to get a little huffy and defensive with me saying that the aides had no health insurance and if they thought that they weren't able to do something safely, then they weren't supposed to do it. She added that as far as the coupons were concerned, if the other aides had clipped coupons for me, they had done it out of the goodness of their hearts because aides were not required to do such trivial things. Perhaps unworthy to her but absolutely vital to me since I could no longer handle a scissors except possibly to stab her in the heart.

Afterward, I thought of telling her I that I guessed that meant that Sandra had no goodness in her heart, but sometimes you think of the best stuff when it's just too late. My argument that aides were there to help their patients with hobbies and activities went unheeded. I asked her how long Sandra had been an aide, and she paused for a long time before she finally said, "For quite a while."

Now I was getting huffy and asked long does that mean?"

And she huffily replied, "For about eight months."

And I knew good and goddamn well that she was lying and this was probably her very first job or at least her first job with an English-speaking person. I got the feeling Grog and Sandra were either related in some way or were fast and furry friends. Grog said she would come with Sandra the next day to interpret what she was supposed to do and see what the problem was.

I was so pissed off at that bitch that I was seething by the time I hung up. How dare she speak to me like that and just dismiss my feelings to take the side of No Habla Inglés.

The next morning, they showed up bright and cheerful. I thought, *Shit, they just ruined a perfectly lovely cup of coffee.*

So I was speaking to Grog and telling her all of my complaints, not looking at Sandra because I was speaking to Grog who told me that Sandra understood every word I was saying. Hah! I had to restrain myself from slapping her in the face, but keep my composure I did. I looked back and forth from Sandra to Grog knowing full well that Sandra didn't have any idea what we were talking about.

Then there was some conversation back and forth in Spanish. For all I knew, they were talking about what a stupid ignorant gringo poop head I was. I asked Grog what they were talking about, and she said that she was interpreting to Sandra the way I needed to have things done; meanwhile, I was thinking, *Why does she need to interpret if Sandra understands every word I say? Right about then I needed Colombo to lean in the door and say "oh, just one more thing."*

Quite authoritatively (I knew Dr. Cinzia would be very proud of me), I told them that I would never have her help me with a shower again because it was just too dangerous and frightening for me, but I would continue to have Sandra's help until Nofi came back from her homeland, which by now, would be just another three weeks—or so I thought.

The next week happened to be Christmas week. I was surprised when Sandra showed up with her eight-year-old daughter. So now I was thinking perhaps she should have called me and let me know or perhaps asked if it was okay to bring her child, which by the way, it was not. No Habla Inglés was not up to par in her communication skills either English nor in Spanish. Anyway, having eight-year-old Maria there turned out to be a really good thing. She spoke perfect English, acted as a translator, and loved to clip coupons; and to tell you the truth, I would much rather have had Maria as an aide than her mother. Don't get me wrong, I liked Sandra as a person and she seemed like a good mother, but as an aide, she really, really sucked.

Alas, Christmas vacation ended, and there was no more beautiful, charming Maria; however, the next time Sandra showed up, she had her little three-year-old son José with her. Cute as a button that kid was, but now I felt like a babysitter. His mama did not bring anything for him to do—no books, no crayons and no toys. When it comes to kids, my heart always melts, so I found him some paper, crayons, colored markers, a pair of kid scissors, and a ruler so he could keep himself busy. I think his mom just expected him to sit on the couch and behave himself the whole time she was there, and that was just not going to happen on my watch. No way, José!

Whenever I took my kids anyplace, I always had a bag stuffed with to-do books, books to read, paper and crayons, and things that they could keep themselves occupied with so they wouldn't be a pain in the ass at a restaurant or at someone's home. Lara's favorite was a giant book of jokes, which kept the family in stitches for hours. She would just stand at the foot of the table after dinner was finished and read jokes from the book. She was seven or eight at the time, and to this day, everyone remembers the joy she brought.

But let me get back to No Habla Engles. While I was getting things settled for little José, I wasn't paying any attention to what his scatterbrained mom was doing. She was going about her way, doing what she always did, so I didn't notice when she had a load of wash going, because the day before, she had done most of it. In actuality, what she had done the day before was to shove two loads of laundry into one load, and when she left, I had to dry two loads myself, which was no easy feat considering that I was in a wheelchair with the use of only one hand and my feet didn't work so well. Dumb is dumb in any language.

Anyway, the extra load of laundry that she did while I was entertaining her little boy consisted of two sheepskin pads for my wheelchair, one velvet dressing gown, one wheelchair seat cover with Velcro to keep it on the seat, and five filthy, dirty microfiber mop cloths that attached to the mop with Velcro, all shoved together in one load.

All of it actually needed to be washed separately. The sheepskin pads were ruined, and there was sheepskin stuck to everything, especially the velvet gown. The Velcro from the wheelchair seat cover was stuck to the Velcro on the mopping cloths, which should only be washed with vinegar in cool water and never with fabric softener and never put in the dryer. So now I was going to have to rewash them myself because they would have a hard time absorbing water. I had explained to her before how to wash microfiber cloths.

And what kind of a bobble head would put filthy, dirty mop cloths in with clothing? A dingbat, that's what kind. A bobble headed dingbat. No Habla Inglés had no common sense. I didn't even tell her about it or complain about it to her because I knew she wouldn't understand anyway. She would just smile, nod her head yes, and say, "Okay, okay," or "I know, I know."

And to top it all off, I have never found the seat cover for my wheelchair and have no idea where she put it. I've looked everywhere, so I am thinking she ruined it and threw it away or took it along with her. I will never know because that was the last day I saw her. Nofi would be back soon, and I just couldn't take any more of her goddamn fuck-ups, which cost me so much more stress and quite a bit more money than if No Habla Inglés hadn't been there at all. I fired her and told her not to come back anymore. Thank you, Jesus!

Like Kenny Rogers says in his song "The Gambler," "You gotta know when to hold 'em and you gotta know when to fold 'em." And I folded 'em. Myself.

22

SCHMUCK

Marlon, a.k.a. my physical therapist, usually called before he came over to make sure I was there and feeling well enough for therapy, so I was a little surprised last Friday when he said he was in a meeting and asked if we could make the appointment for Saturday. Well, I was easygoing and easily adaptable and had no special plans going on for Saturday, so I said, "Sure, that's fine." He apologized again and again. I said, "No problem, don't worry about it," and went on with my ordinary clusterfuck day. I was surprised because at our previous appointment, he'd done the same thing, said he was still in a meeting and asked if we could do it the next day. Fine, fine, not to worry.

I saw Marlon twice a week for about forty-five minutes each time. He made sure that I knew how to spell his name: Marlon with an O, as in Marlon Brando. I guess he did not want to get mixed up with the very large fish. He seemed to be a really nice person, and yet I had no idea that physical therapists had to attend so many meetings. Something didn't seem quite right to me.

Come to find out that the meetings were for some sort of sales promotion thing that Marlon and his wife got shnookered into and were very excited about, so excited, in fact, that he couldn't help himself but to tell me in great detail all about it. He decided to take a break from my physical therapy so that he could concentrate on letting me know about the money-making potential of this opportunity and how successful the speakers were and the stories they told of their vast fortunes. He went fucking on and on and on. I didn't fucking care.

I finally had to tell him to get back to work. While he stretched and pulled and twisted my arms and legs, he told me about this amazing opportunity's website and that I should tell my daughter about it. He said I should call these people and go to the meeting because it was good to share good news with others and to pass on the wealth. I told him of my skepticism but said that I would look into it. I had no idea to do any such thing.

I was concentrating on doing my physical therapy, which is no picnic in the park, but we got through it and finally we were done. While I signed the worksheet, he gave me a few more tips and said that because I was home all the time, it would be easy for me. It would be a great opportunity to make a lot of money, the financial cost to get started was minimal, and yada, yada, fucking ya . . . da. *First of all,* I said to myself, *you patronizing, placating, pathetic little weasel, for a physical therapist to assume that I have nothing to do all day long but sit on my fat, flabby wheelchair-bound ass just waiting for such an opportunity to pop up for me so I won't be so freaking bored because it would give me something to do with all my spare time is just . . .* I'm searching for just the right word . . . fucked . . . that's the word. *It's unethical and borderline criminal and crossing waaaaay over the line from being professional to being a fucking pig.* Yet another caretaker taking advantage of the one he was there to help. I bet he did that to all of his patients—tried to share the wealth and the good news with one and all. Not nice, Marlon, not nice.

Okay, Marlon, see you on Monday.

At 10:15 a.m., the phone rang. It was Marlon, and he was on the way. The first words after the mandatory, "Hi, how are you?" were "Did you get a chance to talk to your daughter about the amazing business opportunity?" that he had so graciously shared with me. I told him no, not really. Once at my house, he had not laid a hand on any of my limbs before he started to tell me about another startling business venture he had found out about when he got a letter from a lawyer. I told him that I had received letters like that before too and that they were scams. I told him that no way, José, would I ever have anything to do with that kind of shit and that he should report that letter to the state's attorney general because it was, in fact, illegal. Besides, the few letters that I had received from the "lawyer" were folded very sloppily and just jammed into the envelope. I had a pretty good feeling that the three Ponzi brothers cooked up this scheme in the basement of their mother's house when they all came over to do their laundry; they had to hurry up and get those letters out before their mother came home from work.

Thank God, my visiting nurse, Pretty in Pink (I called her that because she wore lots of different colored nurses' outfits, but she looked so pretty in pink) rang the doorbell. I introduced them, and pleasantries were exchanged. Pretty in Pink said that she would wait while Marlon the Magnificent did what he did. I interrupted and said that I wanted Pretty to do her stuff first; she was just checking blood pressure, pulse, and breathing and asking bowel-movement questions.

Meanwhile, Marlon looked devastated that his shtick was being interrupted, and now he had to start on what he was obviously very poorly paid to do . . . me. Pretty in Pink stayed for a bit more, watching Marlon as he gloomily went through the motions. Marlon was a fair to middling physical therapist, but now he was etched forever in my mind as a mark, an easy target, not too bright, an airhead, and a schmuck, and although I wish him well, there will be no more gifts of insight or enlightenment, no more Ponzi schemes, three-card monte, finagling, picking my brain, or using me in his pyramid get-rich-quick schemes.

No more Ms. Nice Guy. I mean it. Just maneuver my limbs and joints, help me to get stronger, stretch me, help me to stand up for fifteen seconds while my legs tremble uncontrollably, but *do not* speak unless it concerns your kids or your dog or, God forbid, me. Just do your fucking job, do it professionally, and do it with a smile.

Is—that—too—much—to—ask?

23

Trail of Ants

We are living in a townhouse community that is run by a board of directors. As such, the large yard on the left-hand side of our house is not in the best shape. Whenever it rains heavily—and we have had an awful lot of rain as well as melting snow recently—the ants that are living so happily and abundantly thriving in the many, many anthills on that property are flooded out of their residences and start looking for refuge in the nearest sanctuary, which just happens to be our house. And it just so happens that there is enough food for them here to feed their whole army as well as all of their relatives from far and wide for a very long time.

It seems to me that just one little Oreo cookie crumb can feed a family of fifty ants for at least a week. Now, I'm not saying that we are pigs, and we certainly do try to keep a clean house, but those little bastards can locate anything that does not have a child-safety cap on it or a triple-zipper-sealed plastic bag to protect whatever is in it (or bags from one of those wonderful vacuum-seal machines that will keep anything fresh for up to two years). And so, now *we are at war*. We are bringing in the full artillery, including ant traps, ant-exterminating powders, and of course, the dreaded ant-killing power of Raid! We have now murdered approximately one million of God's little creatures, and we have no sorrow or remorse whatsoever. We had to annihilate so many of them that they could've made a good-sized meatloaf. We were totally schkeeved. They seem to love our dog's food, especially when he has splashed some water into it or we have added a little bit of wet dog food and it is nice and sloppy.

We have had to empty our whole pantry and kill the little fuckers running around in there, back and forth, alerting all within hearing distance that there is plenty to go around, and we have had to throw away so many packages that had the tiniest rips and tears. I pray to God that that will be enough to keep them at bay and we won't, yet again, find a family of ants living in our taco shells.

The communication skills of an ant colony are so extraordinary that it's hard to even fathom. One evening, when Lara and I were watching Nancy Grace on TV, I noticed a steady stream of those freaking ants, one line going one way and another line going in the opposite direction. I couldn't even see what they were so excited about. I mean, it was on the brick wall of the fireplace. I could not see a speck of food anywhere, but they must have found something really yummy, because they were sure going to town. I was stupefied yet again. Goddamn it! I got the vinegar-and-water spray and plastered them all to the fireplace wall because really, they had no business interrupting us during Nancy Grace. Come to think of it, as far as I'm concerned, they are welcome to live outside, but as soon as they enter my domain, they are fair game for hunting.

Lara and I just looked at each other and shook our heads. I finally said to her, "If only the home health care system had even a small percentage of the communication skills of these astonishingly well-organized ants, what a wonderful world this would be."

I have been having a god-awful time trying to get a home health aide who is competent, likable, and honest and who won't take advantage of people needing aid—one of whom is me. After being certified eligible to receive care, which was quite an exasperating process in itself, I chose an agency from a long list that I was given by my state caseworker.

I had no idea how to pick an agency, and the overworked and haggard looking caseworker was not allowed to suggest any. Since I had no idea if there was a rating system available to help, I just chose one because the name sounded so caring and so protective. What a crock of shit.

I had been forewarned by Dr. Cinzia to make sure to set clear boundaries when I finally got an aide. I really didn't see any problem with that. She told me that a lot of people run into trouble with their aides and that setting boundaries about what they are to do and not to do right from the start would prevent a lot of heartache down the road. She told me that it was not unusual for people to go through seven or eight aides before they could find one who was reliable and honest and with whom they were comfortable. I assured her that I would have no trouble, that I would be tough and make sure that I got what I needed and that the right aide would be sent my way. I mean, really, how hard could this be?

Hogwash, the whole lot of it. Inside, I was scared shitless and dreading having a total stranger help me do the things that I really hated to admit I couldn't do by myself anymore. It was a stressful time, yet I learned a lot about relenting and asking for help when I needed it. I was able to push away my ego-based thoughts and learn humility. Most of all, though, I learned acceptance—acceptance of my physical body and acceptance of the help I so clearly needed.

It took another two weeks before the agency finally sent my first home health care aide. Finally, the day came. In just a few days, I would be having my fifty-seventh birthday, and this would be a great start for accomplishing living for yet another year—no small feat. My MS was making things very difficult for me by this time and was putting a great strain on my relationship with my daughter. She was the one who was transporting me in her car back and forth to appointments with medical doctors and Dr. Cinzia, so she had to take off from work quite often. She also went in with me when I had my appointments—my wonderful patient advocate.

The worst part of the whole godforsaken thing was getting me from my wheelchair into the car and then from the car back into my wheelchair. When my appointments were finished, we had to repeat the process and then do it all again when we got home. It was so much work and had gotten so much more dangerous and frustrating that we were just barely hanging on. On more than one occasion, I ended up falling on the ground, and we had to call Life Alert to come and rescue me. Poor Lara was beside herself; she was so worried and so discouraged by everything that she was experiencing as much trauma as I was. The more trauma Lara was feeling, the more I felt, and it was just getting worse and worse. The last time we called for help, I was stuck between my wheelchair and the car. My foot was all tangled up and twisted, and it hurt like hell. It was over 100 degrees, and heat is the dreadful enemy of anyone with MS. Then five or six of our local heroic firemen came to rescue me yet again. I was crying and couldn't stop. I couldn't handle the situation with dignity and grace. But that was the last straw, and I knew that we could never take that chance again. I never wanted to put Lara into a position that was so dangerous for not only me but for my beautiful, darling daughter, who was suffering right along with me.

And now, my aide was coming, and I felt my spirits lifting and my guides guiding, and my guardian angels taking human form. My posse of angels. The cavalry was coming, and help was on the way.

I had spent two days working really hard and pushing it to get the house, in particular my bedroom and bathroom, presentable for whoever was coming. I know it seems ridiculous considering that the job of the aide was to help keep my space clean, but even so, I did not want to be embarrassed by just how filthy it really was getting. I really felt I had to clean before my aide came to help me clean.

And then wouldn't you know it, the aide did not show up. It seems the agency had forgotten to tell the aide that she had a new person to care for. Ants, people, ants! Get it together for the love of God and all that is holy. Still, I kept my cool when I called them, even though it was their responsibility to call me to let me know there was a problem. I had been waiting for the aide and now had to wait a couple more days. What I really wanted to do was to wring their asinine little necks or spray them with vinegar so they would all stick to the wall.

So now it was Tuesday, and I finally met Andrea; who is what we like to call "a big girl".

I call her the Amazon Woman and that description should suffice.

She is at lease 5'11" tall and let's just round it out to 250lbs. And she has very large boobs. Anyway, everything that Dr. Cinzia told me about setting the boundaries from the get-go just went in one ear and out the other. I had not asked her any questions at all about her personal life, and yet I found out that Andrea had a four-year-old daughter named Precious, she is Jamaican, and she was married. As it turned out, I'd find out a lot more about her than I would ever want to know. I should have stopped her at the beginning. I should have been perfectly clear that she was to keep her personal life to herself and not get me involved in any way, shape, or form. That is what I should have done, but as you will see, it is not exactly what I did.

So it was January 20, my birthday, and as it happened every four years, Inauguration Day. I was watching the proceedings on TV. Andrea stopped what she was doing, and she and I watched the inauguration together for a while, each getting a little *verklempt*; it was truly moving. Even though I didn't agree with his politics, it was amazing to see the first black, or at least half black, president of the United States of America.

Andrea helped me to shower, cleaned me all up, lotioned me all over, and blow-dried my hair. It was yummy, and I mean that generically and not sexually, so don't go getting any funny ideas . . . (those of you who fantasize about having sex with those of us with disabilities). She then changed my sheets, cleaned my catheter, gave me a hug, and said, "I'll see you on Thursday." At this time, I was only getting help three days a week for one hour a day.

And so it went, clippety-clop, all going well for several weeks. We were becoming comfortable with one another. She actually got a lot done in that one hour per day. And then it started. She would ask for things, not directly, but in a roundabout way—passive-aggressively, shall we say. Even I could figure out that one. For example, she would say that her allergies were really acting up and she had a terrible sinus headache. Well, I, being a kindly soul who didn't want anyone to suffer, offered her some allergy pills which I found for her and for which she was thankful. And one day, she said she was thirsty, so I told her I had a water machine and she could help herself anytime. Then she asked if I had anything else to drink while she stared longingly at a bottle of Coke I had left on the counter. Ding, ding, ding! I even told her there was ice in the freezer if she wanted some. She got a glass from the cabinet, opened the freezer door, and helped herself to some ice. She then poured some refreshing fizzy Coca-Cola and quenched her thirst. Ahhhhh!

Another day, she noticed the poppy-seed lemon Bundt cake on the counter and asked if she could have a small piece. Not knowing how to say no without offending her, I said yes, so she had her cake and ate it too. After finishing her cake in two huge bites, which made me a little bit nauseous, she told me she was diabetic and really should not be eating cake—so not only was she being a leech, but a very stupid, piggish, and self-destructive leech at that!

Not long after that, she complained that she had not had time for breakfast and she was really in the mood for some soup. Since by this time, she knew the ins and outs of my kitchen and my food pantry, it didn't surprise me that she knew that I had soup. So do you know what I did? I actually went over to our well-stocked pantry, opened the door, and showed her where the soup was. She searched around for a while in there until she finally found some soup she could tolerate, and—hold onto your hats, boys and girls—she asked for some crackers! And dumbass me, I told her they were in there somewhere, so she poked around in there for a while and pulled out the ones she liked—Townhouse, wouldn't you know it?—and sat down to eat her soup. Now, remember, at this time I had an aide for only one hour three days a week. She was eating my soup and crackers during the time she was supposed to be taking care of me. I felt like such a schmuck, but I just didn't know how to take control or put a stop to what was getting more and more manipulative.

Let me tell you, Dr. Cinzia had a field day with this one. Because it wasn't just the one day that she had soup, it was actually three times. I knew I was being manipulated. I knew I was being an ass. It really bothered me, and I felt foolish and taken advantage of. Dr. Cinzia, always compassionate and sympathetic, advised me again and in more detail about setting boundaries. She said that it seemed to be a theme running throughout my life—I allowed myself to be taken advantage of. Light bulbs flashed above my head!

Absolutely, no doubt about it, I was somehow giving off signals that because of my sweetness and my kindness, it was easy to take advantage of me. By now, I was beginning to see how I was letting this happen. I was going to have to grow some balls, get some cojones, develop some stones, stop being a pussy and a pushover, and get tough.

You know how they say that things always get worse before they get better? Now Andrea was telling me that she was getting help from an agency to get her relocated because her lame-ass excuse for a man, not her daughter's father, had threatened her with a gun to her head in front of her little girl. Needless to say, I was aghast. This came out of nowhere. She said she needed references to get to the court stating her good qualities because Lame-Ass Excuse was not going to let her go and said that if he couldn't have her, nobody could. Jesus Christ! Whoa there, Nellie! Now what was I getting hoodwinked into? Way too much information! Does not compute! Meanwhile, she had been using my fax machine and computer to send information back and forth, trying to get this guy out of her life. And how could I say no to her, she being an abused woman and all, not to mention with a little girl for Christ's sake!

Apparently, my balls had not grown very large, or maybe they just hadn't dropped yet, because I wrote that letter for her and it was a damned good one too although she found several things that were not quite right. Geez! I really didn't want that little girl to get hurt and I was sorry to ever have gotten to know so many details about her life! Even though I didn't ask for the information, I should've made it clear from the get-go that I did not wish to know anything about her personal life.

Meanwhile, she had spouted the details out to me as though we were the best of friends. She saw me as such a pussy, such a pushover, and knew that I had a tender heart and really wanted to help people—she just saw me as an easy mark and took full advantage of it. *Bitch*!

Well, the last straw came when she walked through my door supposedly talking to her cousin in Tennessee and asking him for money, for $150. I knew good and goddamn well that her cousin was not on the other end of the line and she was talking to air, making sure that I heard every word. When she hung up from her fake conversation with her fake cousin, I knew he had given her some fake bad news and was not going to send her the fake $150. Quite a setup she had going there, taking advantage of a goodhearted woman with MS in a wheelchair, living in my daughter's home because my only income was Social Security disability. And yes, you guessed it, she asked me for the money, saying that none of her family would help her. I can't imagine why, since she seemed like a pillar of truth and all that was good.

That conniving bitch. That manipulative fucking excuse for an aide. The first thing they learn in their training is not to bring their personal problems into their client's home. Leave it in the car, at a fast-food restaurant, in their toilet, or anywhere else they care to, but not where they are expected to work and care for people in their charge. They are there to make our lives less stressful and less tiring and to leave us more time to do things that we enjoy. Her manipulating ways made my life more stressful and more tiring and left me with less enjoyment than I had before she came along. And that's really saying something.

I finally called the owner of the agency from whence she came and told him the whole story. He was genuinely pleased that I had told them about it and genuinely horrified by the whole discombobulated mess. He kept talking about the soup, which he pronounced "zoop" being of African heritage, Nigerian, I think. "She will have to go. I will fire her. Not to worry, Miss Renae, I have another aide for you, and she will start at the beginning of next week. He talked to me for another ten minutes or so, assuring me that he would make it all right.

The next day, I was shocked when Andrea the Amazon showed up unexpectedly at my front door. Now mind you, she was at least five feet eleven inches tall, and that was without her gigantic wig thing she plopped on top of her head. It added another four or five inches to her height, so you do the math. And to top it off, she had to be at least two hundred fifty pounds, so she was a big girl. I foolishly opened the door without even thinking about it and stood in the doorway for awhile—well, not actually *stood* since I am in a wheelchair—shocked that she was there and listened to her fake crying (there were no actual tears) for a bit before she finally asked me with a little bit of attitude and a slight shift in posture if I was going to let her in, so I did. *Ding, ding, ding!* Alarm bells sounding! Do not panic! Walk slowly toward the nearest exit and leave the building! This is an actual alarm and is not a simulation! Get out now!

At this time, she was telling me, right then and there while she was in front of me, to call the agency owner and tell him that the visiting nurse had lied about her (I had told her about some of the things that Andrea had been doing) and was trying to get her fired. She said the nurse had screamed at her when she told her that she was fired and that if I called the owner back and told him that I still wanted her to be my aide he surely would listen to me. By now, she was very close to me, and I was beginning to feel more than a little intimidated and fearful. I did try to appease her and told her I could not call right then because I was busy doing something else, but I would do it soon.

Seriously—and I am not kidding—she could have snapped my neck like a piece of kindling. She towered over me. She could have done serious bodily harm to me if I didn't pretend to go along with her plan, so I pretended to agree with her on every count. I pretended to be shocked at the nurse's actions and did not let her know that I had already spoken to the owner and that I knew that there were three people listening in on that conversation when she was fired—the nurse, the owner, and the front-desk person—and that at no time was she ever screamed at. The owner told me at the end of our conversation when I let him know of the extent of Amazon woman's naughtiness that he had the other two people listen in so that everyone would know what really happened and they would be witness to my disclosure.

When she was finally ready to go, she came over to me, leaned way down to my level, and gave me a big hug, which could just as easily have been a death blow. I was shaking by the time she left. I immediately called the owner and told him what had transpired.

At my next session with Dr. Cinzia, I read the whole detailed account, which I had written about, and she was properly horrified—not just at Amazon woman's actions but that I had actually let her in the door when I should have told her that this was not a scheduled time and just shut the door in her face. If necessary, I could have called Life Alert for help. The thought never even crossed my mind.

Dr. Cinzia then asked me why I thought I was sent that particular aide. I had to think about that for a minute before I could answer. The first thought that came into my mind was: *What the fuck! Are you fucking kidding me? Why would I choose to have such an unconscionable crazy-ass aide in my home? Geez, Dr. Cinzia, what kind of an asshole do you think I am?* And then it came to me that she had been the perfect aide for me to learn how to handle boundaries. It was a fucking hell of a way to learn. Walking on red-hot coals . . . now that would have been an easier way to learn a lesson about boundaries. That's something I could've easily said "No fucking way" to. You live, and you learn. I was just so happy not to have been mauled or beaten about the head and shoulders by the big, bad Amazonian aide.

It was time to move onto another aide. I would just have to wait and see what sort of creature would be coming through my door.

24

MY MOTHER
WAS NOT A DUSTPAN

Dear Mom,

It's been about fifteen years now since you've passed on, and I am sorry for every bad thought I ever had about you. Now that I am older and wiser and have MS, just as you did, I feel you around me all the time. I feel you when I fall and can't get up and have to call Life Alert to come rescue me. I feel the embarrassment that you felt. I feel the hurt and pain that you felt. I feel the frustration that you felt when you couldn't do what you wanted to do or what you needed to do. I feel your pain and humiliation at the loss of bladder control and having to ask for help to change soaking-wet sheets and smelly catheter supplies and having to be naked in front of people who were taking care of you when you were such a shy and private person.

How were you able to do all that you did? How did you raise six kids, not one of whom has ever been to prison, not one of whom is living on the streets or in a van down by the river, and not one of whom is a serial killer (that we know of)? How did you gather the strength to get up every day and deal with the life you were handed with such a grand sense of humor? Back then, when we were kids growing up, you often seemed harsh with us, and there were times when you just blew a gasket and couldn't take it anymore. And boy, were we in for it then! But now I know it was because we were a bunch of hoodlums and even though we were all really cute, we sometimes got really out of hand. If those six kids had been mine, I would have been in the funny farm a long time ago—either that or in prison for crimes unspeakable.

Remember how you loved to do craftwork and you made Christmas decorations with your kids sitting around the table? In making our own, you showed us how it should be done. You made beautiful Christmas wreaths out of wire coat hangers and plastic bags. You bought paints to use on cloth, and you made beautiful dish towels out of the twenty-pound flour sacks you would cut to the proper size. You taught us to cook and bake, and although your cooking wasn't that great, your baking was phenomenal.

I remember coming home from school almost every day to the smell of homemade bread, cinnamon rolls, poppy-seed strudel, or any number of breathtaking beauties. You also canned beets, corn, and carrots and made homemade jams and jellies, sauerkraut, pickles and relish, and ice cream, prepared the old-fashioned way using rock salt and the hand-cranked ice cream maker with fresh peaches, strawberries, or blueberries and fresh cream from our cow, Bessie. I remember all the vegetables from your humongous garden. I remember pulling carrots from the ground, washing them with the hose and eating them on the spot.

Nothing in the supermarket can ever compare. And you stocked the root cellar with onions, potatoes, parsnips, rutabagas, and other things, and then when a really bad storm was coming or a tornado was advancing, we would all rush to the root cellar with a mixture of great fear and awestruck anticipation.

If we didn't have time to get to the root cellar or it was the middle of the night, you and Dad would bundle us all up in blankets and get us to the basement, to the farthest corner where there were no windows, where the coal that heated our house was stored, and we would wait out Mother Nature's fury, hearing the winds and trees being beaten and mauled and objects of all sorts being thrashed against the house and barns. We would huddle together to keep warm and to give comfort and solace to one another, hardly a word spoken.

There was no need to speak; the noise outside said it all. The storms would pass, we would go back to bed and in the morning, get up exhausted from too little sleep, get dressed, and go off to meet the school bus. If it was summertime, we got to inhale the gorgeous smell of rain and wet earth, excited about the night's near disaster, and life went on as before.

Long after I had moved away from home, there was a tornado that touched down very near to the small town of two hundred people where we went to school, which was twelve miles from our family farm. One farmhouse nearby was completely destroyed, and several family members died. The mother of that group died when a piece of straw went straight through her brain; the end was still sticking out of her head. She was found half a mile away slung over a barbed-wire fence.

Mom, remember when Fuckwad and I came to visit, and we stopped in Bismarck to have lunch and there was a tornado approaching on the other side of the Missouri River? We could all see it when we went outside after lunch. I remember that Dad paid for lunch for everyone, but he didn't believe in tipping and there were a lot of us in our group, so Fuckwad, who was not yet a Fuckwad but still my life partner, stayed behind and added a generous tip while nobody was looking. Still, I was so embarrassed that Dad was so ignorant about the ways of the civilized world.

Anyway, back to the tornado. I think it was Dad who said that tornadoes didn't jump over water, but nobody seemed to be too sure about that. You were in a wheelchair at that time, Mom, and we were all concerned about getting you to safety, not to mention the rest of us. The restaurant had no basement and had a lot of windows. Meanwhile, we and lots of the other patrons were all just standing outside staring in awestruck wonder at this giant force of nature. It was getting closer but was still on the other side of the river separating Mandan from Bismarck. It was as though we were all paralyzed just looking at it. Dad, as the driver, decided that we should all get into the van and head on home, so we did, watching the tornado get farther and farther away from us. Another disaster averted.

I can imagine, Mom, just how helpless you must have felt, not being able to make decisions for your own safety and having to rely on others to wheel you to a safe place, realizing that your wheelchair might very well be a hindrance. Or even a death trap. Well, wasn't that another fine kick in the head? And in addition to all of that, you were scared for the safety of those you love. After all of it was over, we were all so glad to be out of danger and yet exhilarated to have been there to see it. Fuckwad, in particular, was thrilled by the experience, having always lived in New York City. The rest of us had either seen or heard live accounts of tornadoes' deadliness.

In spite of all that you had to do every day, you loved to play board games with your kids and grandkids, especially Scrabble and Aggravation, a game that Uncle Tommy made by hand from a large wooden board. We used different colored marbles as playing pieces. I wonder whatever happened to that game. I'll have to ask Dad if he still has it.

Sometimes, out of the blue, you decided to go for a walk up to the butte, which was about a mile away and got to be a pretty steep climb. You always loved to go there because you wanted to pick wildflowers, which grew abundantly up there. There were crocuses, bluebells, wild roses, daisies, and dandelions aplenty. You would ask whoever wanted to go along to hurry up and put our shoes on, because you were ready and there was no time to dawdle. We all had such thick calluses on our feet from being barefoot most of the time and spending much of our time outside when the weather was nice, but shoes were necessary on this hike because there were cactuses and thistles and lots of prickly things along the way. About halfway to the butte was a little area with extremely fine sand. We would take our shoes off, and we loved to walk and draw pictures and write words in this little bit of heaven. And then we put our shoes on, and off we would go once again.

I remember you falling a couple of times on those trips to the butte. We, as children, did not know that you were ill. We thought it was hilarious and would laugh at you, and you would laugh with us, hiding the pain of not knowing what was wrong with you or why your legs would just all of a sudden give out. Sometimes you needed help to get up again, and now I know exactly what you went through.

There was one time when Ryan, Lara, and I were walking in Manhattan, going to a pizza shop after having gone to Ryan's acting class, and I suddenly fell down onto the sidewalk. My kids had to help me up, and even though they knew that I had MS and I assured them that I was okay, they were heartbroken to see their mom deteriorate. What a difference it would have made if we had known that you had MS; we would have helped you more and would have been much more compassionate.

Yet how could we, because not even you knew, not even Dad knew, not even the doctors knew what was causing your ever-increasing symptoms. Goddamned, fucking, life-stealing MS. Eventually, you lost the ability to do all of your favorite things: reading, gardening, baking, making crafts, and playing games and cards. Your handwriting became unrecognizable, and you were always a letter writer. You were fatigued all of the time and spent much of the day sleeping in a special recliner that Dad bought for you.

And I'm sure that the worst of it was that Dad did not understand that what you were feeling was real, so you tried to hide everything from him. But when it became so apparent and you were finally diagnosed with MS, he built a wheelchair-friendly home for you in the little town of Anittybittytown, North Dakota, population two hundred, where all of your children went to school. You told me over the phone that you hated that idea, that Dad had just made the decision on his own without consulting you, and that it was just one more thing that you had lost control of.

And yet it turned out to be the best of decisions. You now had a home that you could move around in and counters and appliances that were built low enough for your use so that you would be able to keep your independence for a few years longer. You were near your sister Patty and lots of other people in the town who cared for you. They would come to check up on you, usually unannounced, which could be such a pain in the ass because you felt you had to entertain and could not tell them to please go because you just didn't have the strength or the energy to sit down and chat. How amazingly alike we are, Mom! I ache for all that you had to go through.

Dad built his workshop that led from the garage and put in an intercom system so that you could reach him at any time. By that time, Dad had retired from farming and kept himself very busy by refinishing and making furniture and all kinds of other things, including great wooden toys, cedar chests, and grandfather clocks and he made a good amount of money doing what he loved.

The number-one most important thing that came out of all of that was that Dad stayed with you, to help you when you needed him. He told me later that your love for each other kept growing and was so strong that it was impossible to explain and that young people just starting their life together could never, never understand it. Dad's favorite saying is, "There is nothing so bad that you can't find some good in it," and your favorite saying, Mom, was, "What is, is." How very Zen-like for both of you, especially coming from such a Catholic upbringing and belief system. You both sound like a couple of devout monks living in a cave in the Himalayas—certainly, not like the strict German/ Hungarian deeply devout Catholic parents that I knew growing up, who made sure we said the Rosary every night before we went to bed and made sure we went to mass every Sunday.

Dad is now eighty-four years old, and he still works in his shop restoring furniture and making toys to send to children for Christmas. Two years ago, he sent each of us a dustpan made from old license plates with the sides and the back bent up and a wooden handle nailed to the top. Well, just imagine my horror when I opened up the box to find a dustpan made from the license plate of your wheelchair-accessible van, which was a vanity plate with your name, "FRANNIE." What the hell was he thinking using my mother's and his wife's name as a dustpan? You really should see this thing. I showed it to Dr. Cinzia, and she was aghast. Seriously, she's a clinical psychologist, and I don't think even she can figure him out. It turns out that there were two of those FRANNIE license plates, and my sister Rochelle got the other one.

We laughed until we cried when we shared that with one another. I mean, can you imagine using that dustpan with our mother's name on it to sweep garbage into? What would be the implications of that, huh, Dr. Cinzia? Dad told me later that he had run out of other license plates, and then he found those two and thought that we would really appreciate them as a reminder of our mother. At any rate, Mom, don't worry; I'm not using it to pick up garbage or trash or the dog's poop or anything. It's just stuck in a dresser drawer in my room because I can't for the life of me think of what to do with it and I can't bear to throw it out.

Even after your passing, you are still making us laugh and you are still laughing with us. The finest and most rewarding gift that you ever gave to your children was a sense of humor. It takes us far and wide, and being in a wheelchair has allowed me to see the funny side of things at a much slower pace and at a much lower level.

You are my hero, Mom. You carried a very heavy load with grace and dignity, with very little complaint, where many people with disability turn bitter and resentful and unlikable. I strive to be like you, to do for others, to give to others even less fortunate than ourselves, to keep on going when others disappoint or turn their backs on us. You had an inner strength that went beyond your religion and came from your humble and yet magnificent spirit.

I recall you telling me that horrific story about my little brother and his two friends who lived right next door. Dad was in the family room cleaning his gun, which he had not used for quite some time and believed was not loaded. Just as the boys came into the house, the telephone rang and Dad went to answer it. Unbeknownst to Dad, my brother's eight-year-old best friend picked up the gun, just playing around as boys will do, and pointed it at his nine-year-old sibling, pulled the trigger, and killed his brother. These are things you hear on TV or read in the paper but never ever believe it could happen in your family, in your parents' home. I've never spoken to my brother about that incident, and from what I have heard, the eight-year-old shooter blocked out all memory of it. Even now after all these years that story gives me chills.

After a couple of days, Mom, you called on our local priest, who was just up the street in the local Catholic church, because you needed someone to talk to, to give solace, to help ease your pain, and to teach you how to help my then eight-year-old brother get through one of the worst moments of his life. This was many, many years ago, and my brother is now in his forties, but things like this change a person forever.

When you asked Father Francis to come over and speak to you, he refused and said he was too busy; he never called you back, and he never came to visit. What a *fuckhead*! What kind of priest is this? I'll tell you what kind. He was eventually sent away to another parish because of several complaints by preadolescent boys, altar boys he was teaching more than what to do during Mass. The Catholic Church, being what it was at the time and still is, just passed the problem onto another parish, when in fact he should have been imprisoned and castrated in front of the entire congregation. That's just my opinion of course.

At any rate, Mom, I know how deeply hurt and devastated you were when your faith in the Catholic Church betrayed you. We were a deeply Catholic family. We said the Rosary every night, we went to church every Sunday, and for God's sake, we even went to the bingo events to raise money for the church!

Several years after the shooting incident, the family next door moved away. I have never mentioned it to you, Mom, or to Dad, so I really don't know how they coped with their loss or how they got through it, although I do know that the boy's family placed no blame on Dad for leaving a loaded gun around. I still have a hard time absolving him of blame, and I do not understand how he did the unthinkable and did not check or how he could not know the gun was loaded and leave it unattended where anybody could get to it. And yet I know things like this happen every day and cause irreparable harm to everyone they touch. It could just as easily have been my little brother and my dad's son who died that day because of his negligence.

But that was then and this is now. There is nothing so bad that some good won't come out of it. All good things come to me. I am incredibly wealthy.

I miss you, Mom, and I know that you are always with me and that you will be there to greet me when my time on this earth has come to an end.

25

A LETTER TO DAD
AFTER MUCH THERAPY

I don't know where to start writing this letter, Dad. Maybe part of it is because I've been taking amoxicillin for the past five days because of the infected tooth I had to have extracted and I have not been feeling very well. My stomach hurts, I've hardly eaten anything, and I feel nauseous, so I'm just going to stop taking that gut-wrenching drug. It's a fine balance, trying to get everything done so my body is in better shape and managing the effects of all of the drugs that I am taking to alleviate the symptoms of that icky poopy Multiple Sclerosis so that my body works better. I know you know how all that is, Dad, because you were there with Mom through all of her battles, which slowly ravaged her beautiful body and trampled her magnificent spirit.

Dad, I know that your spirit was trampled right along with hers, and I can't imagine what you must've gone through seeing the love of your life diminishing day after day right before your very eyes. You did the best you could all along knowing you had no control over her disease and her slow and painful and self-defeating death, and I am so sorry for your loss. You lay in bed with her when she asked you why she couldn't be like normal people and you told her you didn't know why. After she had gone from us, one of your regrets was that you had not given her a much better reply.

I know how you put medication on the large pressure sore on her backside. Nothing was helping to heal it, and you had to roll her over on her side so you could put that antibacterial salve on her raw wound and bandage it with gauze and tape. It seemed to get a little better for a while and then got bad again, but it never healed and was always painful for her. How awful for you to have to do that to the mother of your children and to see her suffer so much. How she hated for you to have to do that for her.

There was a myriad of other things that you did for her that she hated for you to have to do, and her self-worth and her dignity diminished with each bit of loving care she relented to, having no other option. You had to help her with her catheters and her toileting and cleaning up the messes that her weakened and uncontrollable body left behind. You had to fill out all of the paperwork for the doctors, drug companies, and insurance companies, trying to get as much help as possible to make her life easier. You had to make sure her medications were ordered and she took them every day at the appropriate times. You had to do things to and for your wife that were unmentionable and unimaginable for other people not in your situation.

There were times, Dad, when I was so angry and disgusted with you because I knew how rough you were with Mom; she complained about it often on the phone. I hurt and ached for and with her.

My symptoms were getting worse also, and I was afraid to let them show. You lived in North Dakota, and I lived in New York—a world apart. I could not find a way to tell you to be kinder to her, softer with her, gentler to her. How could I when you were there with her day after day, aching and suffering along with her and knowing somehow that your pent-up anger and frustration were coming out in mean and inappropriate ways. I knew you needed help too; you needed someone to talk to, someone to whom you could say anything and not be judged, but I knew too that there was no way to approach that thought with you. There was no room in your daily hellish mess; you just couldn't see any further than that, and it took all of your strength just to get through each day, just as it did for Mom.

You were in this together, and for that reason alone, Dad, I have so much respect for you. You did what so few men have done; you stayed with a woman with a debilitating disease through thick and thin, in sickness and in health, till death do you part. Statistics show that 80 percent of men will leave when their partner falls ill with MS. There are no words for the strength that it took for you to do that as a man. And I know from personal experience what that meant to Mom. Before I was thinking of you as a mean, cruel, hard man, and now I see you as a hero who stayed with my mother while the ship was sinking. Coming to that realization has crushed all of my negative thoughts against you into miniscule bits, and they have floated out into space where they will enter my atmosphere no more.

I see you now as my elderly father, who did the best he could with the harsh upbringing that he had and a religion that leaves no space for self-forgiveness and furnishes much baggage in which to stuff guilt and self-loathing from the Ten Commandments disobeyed.

With much love and respect, I forgive you, Dad.
Your Daughter,
Renae

26

UNDERWEAR OPTIONAL

Yesterday was totally exhausting. There seems to be very fine line between pushing it, doing the best you can plus a little more, and doing too much so you feel like crap the whole next day.

Marlon (spelled as in Brando), my Filipino physical therapist came to my home and worked me like a crippled mule for about forty-five minutes. Then I had an appointment with Dr. Shah to evaluate me for Botox treatments to help with the stiffness and spasticity in my left side limbs. I had gotten Botox treatments before with another doctor, and they worked wonders for me, making it much easier to transfer and hold onto things, so I did not drop so damn many things, etc., but since her specialty was not in Botox, she thought the best thing for me would be to transfer to Dr. Shah, who was now the newest deputy in my posse.

It took over a year for me to get an opening at the newly opened Southwestern Medical Center for Multiple Sclerosis in Dallas, Texas. The only problem I find at her office is that her nurses are very, very selfish. I asked them to let the doctor know that I wanted her to save a little bit of the Botox to put under my eyes and around some of the wrinkles in my face, and you know what they had the nerve to say to me? They said there was no way they would do that because they were getting all the extras for themselves! I couldn't believe it! I mean, seriously, here I am, the patient who has the insurance to pay for all this crap and they are selfish enough to keep the little extras for themselves. I was wondering why their faces were smiling all the time and even though they were in their forties and fifties their skin was taut and almost flawless—though they could hardly register emotion except for that damn little smile that you couldn't even slap off their eternally friendly little faces. Okay, maybe I exaggerated a little. But I really did ask them and they really did say they kept the extra for themselves. They were, of course, kidding.

So anyway, Dr. Shah pushed, pulled, lifted, and stretched my arms and legs over and over to see how strong I was not and to see my range of motion, which was very limited. As all doctors do, she asked me a whole lot of questions, which I have answered so many times before to so many doctors and most of which I already answered in the preliminary form you have to fill out whenever you see a new doctor. In my mind, this is a total fucking waste of time, but hey, what can you do? Nothing, that's what. Just do what they tell you to do so you can get the hell out of there.

Dr. Shah was recommended to me by my neurologist, Dr. Bates, a wonderful and very caring doctor. Dr. Shah then recommended that I see Dr. Cinzia, my psycho therapist . . . I mean my psychotherapist.

Sometimes the voice recognition program I am using makes up its own funny little language and I have to correct the errors; for example, whenever I say Dr. Cinzia, it always insists on typing Dr. Cynthia and even after training it over and over again, it still insists on doing as it sees fit. I think it might be because I have a lisp. But who knows? It seems this voice recognition program has a very hard time with curse words as well, so I had to train it over and over and over again to type "Fuckwad," which it now reluctantly does, although it insists on underlining it in red to let me know that this really is not the way it should be. Fuck you, voice recognition program. You work for me. I do not work for you.

So anyway, when I told Dr. Shah that I was seeing Dr. Cinzia, she was delighted and raved about her. And the same thing happened when I told Dr. Bates, so as it turns out, they all know and highly respect one another. And all of the above doctors are female, which really delights me. I have a feeling that it is the universe's way of telling me I've got to work on my trust issues with men. Ain't that the truth, Dr. Cinzia?

Anyway, as I was saying, I was exhausted, and my muscles hurt like a mofo. I'll take that as a good sign that my body is getting stronger or probably it's MS doing what MS does . . . fucking me up. I would say "no pain, no gain" but by now, that sounds so trite and common, so I just won't say it.

One more thing about Dr. Shah is that she is very serious and dedicated, which I am grateful for because no one wants a chucklehead for a doctor. She is on the other end of the scale, however, and seems to have no sense of humor whatsoever. When Lara and I were in the office, we cracked jokes with one another every now and then and giggled. That is how we deal with stress: inappropriate remarks and gallows humor. Dr. Shah, bless her heart, just ignored us and did a meticulous workup centered on helping her patient, me, to feel better and move more easily. She is very good at what she does, and she truly cares.

Oh, and one more thing, she asked me if I was able to put on pants or panties. I looked at Lara, and I could see she could not keep a straight face. Neither could I, but I said no, I couldn't do that anymore, still wondering where this was going. She said to make sure when I came for my Botox sessions to wear shorts or something, because she was going to put Botox injections in my left upper thigh and my leg as well as my left arm and hand. Lara and I looked at each other once again, giggling as I assured Dr. Shah that I would do as she asked. Apparently, she did not want to see even the tiniest hint of pubic hair. I really didn't blame her considering I hadn't been doing very much gardening down there lately—well, actually for a long time; there had been no man in my life to see that particular overgrown area since I'd been in a wheelchair. So let's just say that my shrubbery is a little unkempt but at least the neighbors can't see it.

One of the perks of my particular disability (ha ha) is how freeing it is not to have to wear a bra or panties, because I literally cannot do that anymore. It bothered me for a while, and I struggled with it. I bought all kinds of different underwear, but none of it was easy enough for me to put on with just one hand, so I just gave it up. It's one more thing I don't have to worry about. It's quite amazing, really, once you accept your disability, how easy it is to give things up and how other things come in and fill up that space. The time you spent in the struggle to do things is freed up, so that if you just relent and realize you don't have to do it, then your real self starts to show up in little ways and then in bigger and bigger ways.

You realize that no one really cares what you are wearing when you are in a wheelchair and that you really are free to say and do outlandish things that you otherwise might not because there is no protocol or accepted mode of behavior for people with disabilities or, for that matter, for people with serious illnesses of any kind, physical or otherwise.

There is a freedom that comes with disability; when you accept who and what you have become, you are able to let go of so much garbage that is just so unimportant in life. You leave more and more space for good and for peace and for seeing things because you move at a much slower pace and are closer to the earth—things you would never notice before, you now see in a brand-new way. Instead of fighting against and pushing against that huge brick wall that is your disability, whatever that may be, I have found that just relenting to it takes away the power that it has in your negative thinking; you can replace it with something positive and giving in the spirit of love. Even a smile or a handshake or a pat on the back will leave a much better impression and a much better feeling than a frown or a complaint or a nasty attitude.

When you are in a wheelchair, you can really pay attention to people and their actions and attitudes and their rushing around. When I am waiting for my bus and just sitting in my wheelchair outside, almost everybody smiles at me and says hi; some of them quickly and uncomfortably so they don't have to be confronted with someone else's visible disability. A few people will stop and ask if I'm okay and if my ride is coming. A few even stop to chat for a while. I find that most people are good, and yet I am always careful because of those few clunkers who prey upon those who are weaker than they are.

Which reminds me, there was a time when I had been living in Dallas for several years and my daughter, Lara, came to live with me. I was driving back and forth to work every day, and one evening, I got out of my car clumsily and started walking with my cane to our apartment. I came to about twenty feet away from my front door when two young girls, who looked as though they were about sixteen or seventeen years old, came up behind me; one stood at my side, and the other had something sticking in my back. One of them said she had a gun and if I did not give them my small leather backpack, which I used as a purse, they were going to kill me. They kept saying it over and over, "We will kill you. We will kill you!"

Meanwhile, I was doing my best to get the backpack off of me, which was hard because I had to keep hold of my cane or I would fall. I kept telling them over and over, "Relax, I'm getting it for you." But apparently, I was not nearly fast enough for them. They pushed me on the ground and very forcefully tore the backpack from me, wrenching my arm in the process. These were beautiful-looking young women with matching shorts sets, and I would never have believed by looking at them that they could act so brutally.

It was about 6:30 in the evening, still daylight because it was summertime, and usually there were people coming home from work or walking their dogs or standing around talking outside. But this day, there was no one around. The two punk-ass bitches ran away, but there was no way that I could see where they went. I was lying on the sidewalk, not able to stand up, and bleeding on my hands and knees where I had been pushed. Thank God I had my keys in my hand when I was assaulted by that juvenile delinquent duo. And I mean that in a bad way. I saw my keys were laying a good ten feet behind me. Even back then, my left side was very weak and numb, so very slowly and painfully, I had to maneuver my body back to get the keys and then turn around and go back to get my cane. I tried over and over, but I just could not get up again, so I crawled with my right side dragging the left side of my body along until I finally got to my front door. Still, there were no people around. Again and again, I tried to stand up so that I could reach the keyhole and open the front door, and finally, I was able to reach up just enough to unlock the door.

I crawled into the house and shut the door with great difficulty, because by now, I was so exhausted, I got to the couch and was able to lift myself up and sit down. I called 911, and within ten minutes, two police officers were there. Lara was out shopping, so I called Ryan and his dad, and they came immediately. I didn't break down until people started to show up, and when the crying started, I couldn't stop. It was clear that those two little shits had been watching me for some time and knew my schedule. And what better person to victimize than someone with a disability? Easy prey.

Ryan's dad called my bank and all my credit card companies and got that whole mess straightened out, which was a total relief because I was too much of a mess to deal with any of it. I explained to the policemen what had happened and which direction I saw the hoodlums run, and they said they would scour the neighborhood, but it was very unlikely that they would ever be caught. They never were.

Lara came home a short time later, utterly shocked and horrified because she had just left five minutes before I was mugged.

I took off from work the next day and found out that someone had tried to use my credit cards already, and I was very grateful for the help I had received.

I was really shaken up. I did not hear them come up behind me, nor did I see them anywhere in the vicinity. I was always aware of my surroundings, so there was no way I could have avoided this attack. I had remembered hearing advice from an expert to try to keep your assailant calm, do what they tell you to, and don't attempt to fight. I did all of the above and was just so thankful that I hadn't been shot or beaten or hurt badly. The worst that happened was that I lost some trust in mankind—I was a very trusting person—and I lost the sense of being safe in my own home.

Well, that was quite a detour I hadn't expected to make. That's why writing for therapy is so important to me. It helps me to remember and to assimilate and to put behind me the things that have traumatized me and have taken parts of me away. And then I can put the pieces back together the way they make sense again.

27

So Long, Mate

Before Fuckwad was a Fuckwad (not his real name), he used to tell me, as he held me tight and looked lovingly into my eyes, that I was his soul mate and we were deeply connected. Little did I realize, little could I even imagine, that one day he would be my so long mate and our deep connection would be cut to the core, amputated, sliced off with no anesthesia and nothing to stop the bleeding, leaving endless day after motherfucking endless day of pain and anguish.

Now I am no longer trying to figure out how I could have stopped it—if I had paid more attention to the signs, listened to the whispering voice in my head, trusted myself—and saved my marriage so I would still be Mrs. Fuckwad. But now there is a different Mrs. Fuckwad, Mrs. Margo Fuckwad (not her real name).

I was so deeply disturbed, disrespected, disapproved of, dissatisfied with, distanced, disgraced, dampened, disempowered, damaged, disgusted with, disagreed with, and finally divorced. Now I think back to all the tiny whispers getting louder and louder until I was battered with disses every single day and in my dreams every single night and realize it all came from you, Fuckwad. But it was absorbed by me, into me, into my very being, and it slowly and sadly changed who I once was.

It took thirteen years of hoarding all of that negativism in my being, all of those nightmares, for me to finally take that first step to get help, to find my spiritual self once again, to start hearing whisperings of "Renae, you are a child of God. You are special. You're lovable. You deserve all that is good. The past is gone; it was there for you to learn from; you had to listen to the whispers to be aware of your goodness." When I fall into the old trap of negative thinking, I stop and become aware of it and think of all that is positive in my life. We all materialize, prosper, pray, meditate, learn, and grow into what we are meant to be: spirit, serenity, peace, love.

So long, Mate . . . Peace be with you.

28

LESSONS I HAVE LEARNED IN 2010 AND CHANGES I WILL MAKE IN 2011

When I first started therapy over a year ago, I went with the intention of becoming better able to deal with MS and to understand how I had lost the sense of who I really was. What I realized, thanks to all the hard work I have done with Dr. Cinzia, is that what I needed to learn first and foremost was how to deal with life and understand why I made the same mistakes over and over. I needed to learn how not to feel like a victim and to be a doer wherever the course of life took me. I started with self-consciousness about having MS—the stumbling, the bladder control stuff, the terrifying progression of this godforsaken motherfucking disease. Not wanting to admit that I am sick and that MS is incurable and all the fear, terror, desperation, and stress of trying to hide it from everyone are themes I have lived since my diagnosis. But now I am hiding no more.

The irony is that those of us with MS should avoid stress in our lives as much as possible. Whoever said that surely did not have MS and probably lives peacefully on a tropical island without a care in the world, just sitting under a huge umbrella drinking tropical drinks from a coconut shell and enjoying the sound of the waves going in and out, in and out, in and out all fucking day long. Avoid stress, my ass! If you look up MS in the dictionary, one of the synonyms is the word *stress*, so don't go giving me that bullshit 'cause I ain't buying it!

After only a couple of sessions of therapy, I realized I had even bigger fish to fry, and before I could get past all of the negative, life-paralyzing, nightmarish stuff of having MS, I was going to have to look first at how my view of myself and the world was formed and the lessons learned along the way that have shaped the way in which I deal with MS, the way I think about myself, and all of the wonderful things I can do in spite of it.

In particular, I needed to look at the relationships I'd had with the men in my life—Daddy Wad, Ray Wad, Cheapwad, and especially Fuckwad. I've spent lots and lots of time thinking about, writing about, and talking about . . . Fuckwad.

I can now see how guilt has been the basis of many of my decisions. I can see that much of my self-loathing and self-disgust comes from not speaking up and not being my true self but instead bending and twisting to be what I thought those men wanted from me. How much happier and more self-satisfied I would have been if I had followed my own dreams instead of supporting the dreams of the Wads. I feel that I've come such a long way and yet have so far to go to be able to relax and not stress about things that I feel need to get done or things that I should be doing. I'm getting much better at that. When I feel anxious about one thing or another, I stop and repeat my mantras over and over:

I am incredibly wealthy.

All good things come to me.

As the layers of ugliness slough off of me, I find I have more physical energy, which allows me to be a contributor to our household and not to be so much of a burden. And as I feel better, I can do more good for others who are in worse conditions or situations than I am. The amount of work, thought, and energy that it takes for me to collect my coupons, get them organized, make travel arrangements so I can go shopping, and box everything up so that the homeless abused women and children will be helped by my actions is what keeps my mind active and gives me a sense of contributing to society and making a difference in someone else's life.

Those who are homeless or beaten and abused and literally have to flee for their lives are the ones I feel an affinity with. I want so much to give at least a little of the joy and fun and self-respect that everyone deserves. The bravery of that action, of getting safely away from their abusers, is astounding, and the people who give them a safe place to sleep, shelter, safety, counseling, comfort, and solace, who are there to stop the cycle from repeating itself yet again, they are the heroes. And I want to do my small part to help in their cause.

And yet I know there is so much more that I can do.

So for the coming year, I will work hard at physical therapy. I will write more. I will read more. I will write a book about MS from my personal experiences and include some of the funny, ironic things that come from hardship. I will not be a victim or be victimized. I will make my voice heard. I will do things that I am afraid to do. I will not procrastinate or use MS as an excuse just because I am afraid to try new things. I will think big and not beat myself up when I backtrack or need help or feel weak and small. I will see that the people who come into my life are all there to teach me something whether it is good or uncomfortable or downright lousy. I will do the best I can. I will rest when I need to, and I will eat well. I will get out into the world more and experience life and the things that I love to do. And I won't feel guilty when I need to sleep a lot. I will not think of all the time I wasted not doing what I thought I needed to do. I will listen to my body. I will live a more Zen like life. I will meditate more. I will live a more spiritual life, and that will be *my* fucking priority. My belief is that we are here on this earth to learn lessons from the hardships that come our way (i.e., fucking MS) (and fucking Fuckwad that fucking fuck of a motherfucker!).

Dr. Cinzia says we still have more work to do concerning Fuckwad. No shit, Sherlock!

> All good things come to me.
> All good things come to me.
> All good things come to me.
> I am incredibly wealthy.

29

MURDERED BY THE MOB

The article that follows is an astonishing true story about the man who shot my ex-father-in-law's best friend, Louie DiBono, in one of the underground parking garages of the World Trade Center Building Number One in New York City. Louis's wife was also the best friend of my ex-mother-in-law, who died last year. My ex-in-laws, Fuckwad's mom and stepdad, Lillian and Bob, met on a blind date where they were introduced to one another by Louie and his wife Jane.

I remember Lillian telling the story of how they were at dinner as a foursome on their first date; the steam from the soup she was eating loosened one of her false eyelashes, and it fell into her bowl. I still giggle when I think of her telling that story. She was a beautiful woman, spunky, full of life, and the glue that kept the family together. To this day, Lara considers Bob and Lillian to be her grandparents and goes to visit them several times a year. It was love at first sight when they first met each other when Lara was just a little girl of six years. They embraced us, loved us, scooped up Lara and me, and made us a part of their family. And that is how I came to know the DiBonos.

At that time, Louie was not involved in the Gambino family. Both Louie and my ex-father-in-law were in the construction industry, which was coming more and more under the control of the Mafia. Louie took one path, and my ex-father-in-law, thank God, took another. Even though he had to fight tooth and nail to get construction business and made a lot less money, he kept his integrity and is alive today at the age of ninety, still loved and respected by anyone who has ever had the privilege of knowing him.

The following posting was made in September of 2008 and is just one of the theories of why Louie DiBono was one of the reported nineteen murders committed by Sammy "the Bull" Gravano.

> Louis DiBono ran a drywall and plastering company, and was a Gambino soldier. On several occasions DiBono and Salvatore Gravano requested permission from various mob bosses to have each other killed over various business disputes. On several occasions these disputes were resolved without violence.
>
> Gravano approached Gotti about killing DiBono when DiBono had neglected to pay taxes on his businesses. Gotti decided to take over DiBono's businesses, and ordered a meeting between the two. When DiBono repeatedly refused the order and didn't show, Gotti ordered the hit on DiBono. Gotti's associates made several attempts to meet with DiBono to carry out the hit but he never showed. Around this time DiBono had secured a contract to work on the WTC. So when Gotti's associates

became aware of this fact, they knew where to find him, and ultimately, end his life.[2]

This next article concerns the amazing stupidity of the psychopathic serial murderer who wreaked so much havoc and devastation in our little corner of the world.

Mafia Hitman, Salvatore "Sammy the Bull" Gravano—whose testimony helped send crime boss John Gotti to prison for life—was arrested Thursday in Phoenix for his role in allegedly financing a drug ring that supplied the drug Ecstasy to the area's burgeoning "rave" scene, police said.

Gravano, his wife, daughter and son were among 35 people arrested in early-morning raids around the Phoenix metropolitan area. Authorities said the former under boss of the Gambino crime family was the group's financial backer and that Gravano effectively controlled the market of the designer drug in the state.

Authorities said the ring is connected to a white supremacist gang known as the Devil Dogs, so-named because members bark as they assault victims.

The gang is made up of young, white males from mostly middle-class families based in suburban

---

2 John Marzulli and Tracy Connor NY Daily News

Gilbert. At least eight of those arrested Thursday were affiliated with the gang, officials said.

Sgt. Jeff Halsted, a spokesman for the Phoenix Police Department, said the drug organization peddled as many as 30,000 Ecstasy pills a week and each pill had a street value of up to $30. The pills, which contain methamphetamine, look like candy and are stamped with symbols such as the Nike swoosh and Christmas trees, Halsted said.

Gravano—who has admitted to ordering or committing 19 murders—has been living in suburban Phoenix in semi-seclusion after his turncoat testimony in Gotti's blockbuster trial in New York City. His testimony in 1992 allowed federal officials to convict Gotti, a mob boss who in three previous trials had been acquitted and come to be known as the "Teflon Don."

In return for his testimony, Gravano cut a deal with prosecutors that allowed him to serve five years for racketeering.

Gravano cut a dashing if brutal figure and managed to charm many in law enforcement. During his sentencing the judge noted positive comments from federal officials and concluded that Gravano had "irrevocably broken with his past."

He was in the limelight again when author Peter Maas recounted his story in the book *Underboss*, later made into a television movie. He entered a federal witness program but dropped out in 1997, proclaiming he was not afraid of being the target of a hitman. Gravano was living under an assumed name and had installed his family in a sprawling home in Tempe.

Gravano was charged Thursday with conspiracy to distribute dangerous drugs and is being held on $5 million bond. His family members were arrested on the same charge, as was Mike Papa, described by police as the co-founder of the Devil Dogs. According to one law enforcement official, Papa recruited his associates "for the purpose of intimidation[3]

Quite a little family business they had going there, unbeknownst even to their closest neighbors. How fucking stupid and arrogant was he to have gotten away with at least nineteen murders but turned down witness protection and then go ahead and create a gigantic illegal drug ring by organizing, manufacturing, and distributing Ecstasy pills with cute little pictures of Santa on them?

There was a time when my ex-husband worked for Louie DiBono's company as a marble cutter and installer in the World Trade Center buildings, but that job went kaput with Louie's murder. My ex and I attended Louie's funeral, which was absolutely packed, and there were a lot of people there that we did not know—and more than likely, we were very lucky that we didn't.

---

3   From Wikipedia, the free encyclopedia Sammy Gravano.

For some reason, which I will never understand—call it fate or serendipity or what is, is—I ended up sitting in a chair next to Louie's wife while they played a special song she had requested for him, in his honor, "You Are the Wind Beneath My Wings" by Bette Midler. She really did love him, and that song apparently had special meaning between the two of them. Almost everyone in the room was crying or had tears in his or her eyes, and I wasn't sure if I should take hold of her hand and try to comfort her or just let her grieve in peace. I took her hand lightly, and she returned in kind keeping her amazing composure as she always had. I have always loved her regal stature, her amazing beauty, and her awesome sense of humor. I can't even imagine the hell that she had to go through after Louie's death. Her home was invaded by federal agents, she was in fear for her life from the Gambino family, and she was interrogated over and over again. Eventually, she left New York, but she never lost touch with Lillian and Bob.

For Louie's fiftieth birthday, his wife gave him a surprise party to which we were invited. The house was gorgeous with a huge outdoor deck and a sunken swimming pool, a two-story hand-cut marble fireplace, a kitchen fit for royalty, and a live-in cook and maid. The party was wonderful, and Louie was one of those bigger-than-life characters.

He was boisterous and intimidating even though at that time we did not know of his connections. He seemed genuinely surprised by the party as he walked in with his golf clubs being carried by his chauffeur, who, it is rumored, bought and snorted cocaine with him. I've never known anyone before who had live-in help and a private chauffeur; however, my ex had grown up as a little boy with them doing very special things for him. So it is no wonder that everyone in the family took the news of his death and how it all came about so devastatingly.

Our whole family was deeply affected by the death of Louie DiBono who was *murdered by the Mob.*

30

ONCE A FUCKWAD, ALWAYS A FUCKWAD

One morning, when Ryan was about ten years old, Fuckwad took him to school and came back to our apartment building to pick me up. He didn't want me to go to work that day, but for some reason, I needed to be there. By then, I had a really hard time walking, and even with my cane, it was very difficult. I had a tough time getting into the car, and Fuckwad didn't lift a finger to help me. He resented the hell out of having me around; I embarrassed him. He never had a kind word for me anymore, and the harder I tried, the worse it got.

On that particular morning, he was especially cold and mean. The trip from home to our store took about fifteen minutes, and the whole time he was screaming at me about my worthlessness, my laziness, my not being conscious and not being present so he had to take care of everything himself. He pointed his finger at me and looked at me with disgust. He told me he would take Ryan and just leave me there, living on the street, or I should just go live with my dad, the crazy old man. I cried unstoppably the whole way. I was trapped in a small space with nowhere to escape. I was stunned with grief and disbelief that he could do this to me. I was at his side for all those years through the tough and scary times of his addictions to pot and gambling. I couldn't fathom where or how things had gotten to be like this.

When we finally got to the store, he had to park on the opposite side of the street. He sat there for another ten minutes lecturing and berating me, not caring at all how frightened and stunned I was, not caring if anyone was watching. He finally stormed off, slamming the door behind him. I sat there sobbing, retching with pain for half an hour. I finally hobbled across the street and went into the store, in front of all the people milling around, thinking they could see how horribly he had treated me and how pathetic the whole scene was. I just wanted to be invisible so no one would see the world I was living in. The world where multiple sclerosis turns everything insane and where nothing makes any sense. I was humiliated that my husband took such little regard for me, his wife who is sick with an ever increasing and incurable disease. That even in public he found it to be righteous behavior to beat me senseless with his words.

He wouldn't even help me across the very busy city street. My face was red and swollen from crying. I was mortified, humiliated, not knowing what to do or how to reclaim my dignity. I struggled up the twelve stairs, counting each one as I went, as I always did. I went to the bathroom and got myself together as best I could, and then I went downstairs and started to wrap merchandise that we had sold online on our website, for which I was responsible. I took the photographs, cropped them, and wrote the descriptions of the items, and then posted them to the proper section on the website; it was work that I loved doing and was very successful with and good at.

That was the day I discovered the phone bill and all the calls to Texas. There were hundreds of calls, all to the same number. Fuckwad caught me looking at the bill and let me know in no uncertain terms that I had no business opening his mail, that it was his store and I had nothing to do with the business, and that it was no concern of mine what those calls were or whom they were sent. And once again, he turned the situation around and made it look like I was the one who had erred. He was a master at manipulation and making someone else look like the bad guy. And in this case, I was the one who was made to look as though I had done something really terrible.

I left at 2:30 to pick up Ryan at school, putting on a happy face for my little boy.

There were several times when Fuckwad told me he had a job opportunity in Minnesota and was going on a business trip to meet with the owners to look at properties. This was the time just before I found out that he was a Fuckwad. I fell for it hook, line, and sinker, helping him pack, ironing his clothes, shining his shoes, and even cutting his hair. He bought new clothes—shirts, underwear, and socks—to appear appropriately for his exciting opportunity. When I asked for it, he said he didn't know the phone number or the name of the hotel but he would call me and let me know. He told the same lie to his mom, his best friend, and our employees.

So while he was in Texas making love to his mistress, I took care of the store and our boy.

When he came home, he said it went really well, and I was so proud of him. Although his story had a lot of holes in it, not for one moment did it register to me that he was fucking lying. He said he had to go a couple more times to solidify things and that this new company was paying for everything. I couldn't have been prouder that it was really coming together.

Motherfucking, son of the devil, Fuckwad. I had no clue.

Once I knew about Fuckwad's girlfriend and that he was talking to her late at night, I lay in bed crying myself to sleep. The bedroom was right next to the living room where he talked to her for hours via phone or computer, sometimes until 3:00 or 4:00 in the morning. By then, my spirit was so deflated I couldn't even defend myself. All I wanted to do was sleep. I didn't want to get up. The depression was so overwhelming; I thought of suicide many times, always as a last resort. It was a comfort knowing that if things got to be so bad I couldn't handle it anymore, at least I could put an end to it. Only my kids kept me alive. I couldn't do that to them.

After Ryan left for school and Fuckwad went to work telling me I wasn't needed that day, I often masturbated just to relieve the pressure, crying even during orgasm.

One day, I forgot to put my vibrator away and left it on the bed. Fuckwad saw it lying there and dragged me in to see what I'd done. He screamed at me and castigated me with venom oozing out of his mouth and slowly poisoned me with his cruelty; what if Ryan came in and saw that out in the open? How would I explain that to him? How could I be so fucking ignorant? So not present? I felt like a total failure, humiliated once again.

And the worst part of it was the fact that Fuckwad told all of this to his mother. I guess he had to prove he needed to divorce me; he needed to tell her how crazy I was, how negligent, how stupid, anything to take the spotlight off of his deceitful, lying ways. I felt so betrayed. I didn't say anything bad to any of his family about Fuckwad. I loved them, and now they were against me too. He totally isolated me. And I never once spoke badly to Ryan about his father. I had nowhere to go, and I was not going to risk losing my son.

One thing after another, it never ended; there was no relief. He kept telling me I better get a lawyer because I didn't deserve to have Ryan and that I was an unfit mother, and if I didn't shape up, there would be harsh consequences. He said that something really bad would happen. By then, I had actually become really afraid of him. What was he planning? Was it all just talk, or was he really planning to harm me in some way—maybe even have me killed if I didn't just disappear and be out of his life forever? His threats had escalated yet again.

I finally did get a lawyer. He turned out to be a legally blind lawyer. I was just blinded by confusion, loss, and utter devastation. And then one day, I just couldn't take it anymore. I called my blind lawyer, and he advised me to get a court order to keep Fuckwad away from me. It took me almost a full day in court to do that. My blind lawyer then told me to go to the bank and take out as much money as I possibly could because I just might need it. I did. There was about $2,500 in the business checking account, and I took it all out. I made arrangements for Ryan to spend the night at his friend's house. As I was walking down the sidewalk, I happened to meet J., who looked traumatized, as though something bad had happened.

Fuckwad had learned that it was J. who had told me about his affair, and again, he had turned the tables making J. the bad guy because he had broken the man's code of honor, which apparently, according to Fuckwad, was that men never tell of another man's indiscretion. So J. was out of a job, and he said that Fuckwad was at home with Ryan. He was apparently waiting for me to come home and face the music. I cannot tell you how terrified I was to do that.

As per my blind lawyer's advice, I called for a police escort to take me to our apartment. Two policemen arrived while I was standing there trying desperately not to fall in the street. I got in the police car, and they drove me home. Several people at the apartment building as well as our doorman saw us entering the building and going up to the fourth floor in the elevator.

I had no choice now; there was no turning back. I unlocked the door and went into the apartment with the policemen a few steps behind. They told Fuckwad to gather a few things and that he needed to leave. J. had told me that Ryan was there but I had no time to change plans. I had not expected my son to be there, nor his best friend, Mark. I had made arrangements for the boys to be at Mark's house.

But there they were. My poor little boy was stunned and crying hysterically, not knowing what was going on or why the police were taking his daddy away. Needless to say, Fuckwad was beyond words; he could not believe what was taking place, that I had the balls to do this—to actually get a lawyer, go through the courts, and get some space from him. He went into the bedroom and got a few things, and the policemen took him away. But what I had not counted on was that my son would have to go through this, and it is one of the most regretful times of my entire life. I had planned it to go differently so that Ryan would not be traumatized by this whole mess, but that was not the way it turned out.

I found out later that Fuckwad's family thought that I had him taken out of the house because I was bitter about his affair. They had no idea what I was going through, and I never told any of them. They were my family too, and I didn't want to do anything that would hurt them, especially his mother and his stepfather.

When Fuckwad was gone, I held Ryan and told him everything was going to be okay and that it would all work out. I knew that by then the grapevine was spinning, but it was too late to stop the inevitable. I have no idea what would have happened if I had not shown up with the police.

Blind lawyer advised me to change my locks, which I did. I had taken a giant step toward defending myself, and as freeing as it felt to have done that, I was dumbfounded about what to do next.

After two days, Fuckwad called, amazed that I had the chutzpah to hire a lawyer. I reminded him that he told me that I had better get one. He was speaking to me in a very calm and somber way. There was no name-calling, no cruelty. He said he really wanted to come back home, and I told him that I was afraid of him and that he could never ever speak to me like that again, that I just couldn't take it anymore, and that things had to change. He was very chagrined and spoke to me calmly and regretfully, so I relented and he came back home.

Two days later, Fuckwad called me into the bedroom where he and Ryan were lying on the bed hugging, and Ryan was crying. I came into the room, and Fuckwad said to me, "Look at him! Look what you did!" I was standing there, leaning on my cane, not knowing what to say. I just stood there and took it all. I absorbed all of the disgust and pain and hurt, not saying anything to defend myself because I knew it would be so much worse on our son for me to try to explain what I had been through to take such dramatic steps as to call the police and get a restraining order. All I could say was that I didn't think that Ryan was going to be home and that I never meant to put him through this.

I have no idea what Fuckwad told our son while I wasn't there, but it must've been a hell of a story, because Ryan was very angry with me, so angry he spit at me. Fuckwad took him in his arms and comforted him. He got to be the good daddy, and I was a very poor excuse for a mommy. And this is just a couple of days after I had let him back into the house, so now he was turning my son against me.

All during this horrific scene, Fuckwad was looking at me as though I had done irreparable harm to our child. And I felt that way too. I was horrified that Ryan had been there when the police took his dad away. Inside, I was screaming, "You motherfucking piece of shit! You created this! You were the one who hurt our child. You were the one who verbally abused his mother, the mother of your child. You are the liar, the cheat, the bastard who wasn't man enough to be honest with me and take ownership but turned it around so it looked like I was the one who caused the whole fucking mess!"

I took the blame. I said nothing when Ryan spat at me. I said nothing when Fuckwad blamed me for the whole fucking mess. I felt so helpless; I couldn't even comfort my child. I had to leave the room aching inside, not even standing up for myself because that would mean that I would be putting my child's well-being at risk. The last thing I wanted to do was cause a rift between Ryan and his dad or between Ryan and me, and it took all my strength not to start a screaming match and to put Ryan in the middle of a tug-of-war, using him as a pawn.

He has grown up to be a very fine young man, and if I have ever done anything good, it was to protect him from having to choose sides and to hear hateful, cruel words from either one of his parents about the other. I don't think that he ever even heard any of the foul mouthed things that his dad said to me. And that was the way I wanted it to be. I have always wanted Ryan and his dad to have a wonderful relationship, and they do. And my relationship with Ryan is wonderful as well.

Afterward, they came out to the living room. Fuckwad had smoothed everything out so we could move forward.

I prayed every night for the strength not to love him anymore. And slowly, I was able to let go of him and try to put one foot in front of the other, weak and wobbly as they were, and just do one task at a time. Any more than that was just too overwhelming. One day at a time was even too much; I just went from one thing to another and on to the next, working on all of the details I was going to have to take care of to make this separation. I still loved him, but I did find the strength to let him go once I finally learned the whole truth. The truth will set you free, so they say. I was able to set Fuckwad free, and yet for me, it has been thirteen years since our divorce, and I am just now setting myself free from the shackles of the past.

Finally, I am able to sleep with only occasional nightmares, without reliving the incidences of injustice over and over in my head. A great weight has been lifted from me as I shed the layers of sadness and grief so that now my writings only concern the troubles I bear from the here and now, and I am able to bury the past. The clusterfucks go hand in hand with MS and with life in general. The best way I know how to cope with anything is with humor and sometimes that means it's pretty damn raunchy but still pretty fucking funny.

Life is pretty fucking funny, and when you're in a wheelchair, you are low to the ground and you move pretty slowly, so you can see things from a different perspective than able-bodied people do. Don't get me wrong, life is not a bowl of homemade minestrone soup. And lots of times, it's just a pile of shit, which I have to clean up myself because apparently I forgot to send in some important renewal papers to Medicare, so now I have to wait up to forty-five days to get a home health aide again. That means doing a lot of things myself again, and to add injury to insult, my electric wheelchair has broken down and I have to wait two weeks for the parts to be ordered. Fortunately, I have a backup, but it's not nearly as comfortable as the other one. I am getting pressure sores, and also, it doesn't raise and lower, so again, I am asking for more help. And that just sucks.

Now when I think of Fuckwad, I don't feel like a victim, I don't cry, I don't think hateful things about him or about what he has done to me. I'm still not totally free of my history but in the past year and a half, I have come so far. I was feeling such guilt, trauma, pain and feeling sorry for myself having to live in a wheelchair. I started with just very sloppy writings on various pieces of paper for my therapy sessions. Now, I'm putting them into a compilation that I hope will give some solace and inspiration to others, abled or disabled. Because when you think about it, everybody's disabled in one way or another, and those are the things that we can learn the most from. Some disabilities are on the inside where we can't see them and some, like mine, are visible to all.

There are people who are just so grumpy and morose and depressing to be around that I would rather be in a wheelchair than to be like that. You know who you are, so get your head out of your ass and buck up. Go clean out your closet and donate your discards to Goodwill or volunteer a little of your time to do something good for someone who has worse problems than you do. The best prescription for getting out of a slump is to do something good for someone else.

To tell you the truth, the best thing that I ever did for myself was to seek help from Dr. Cinzia. I love the saying "When the student is ready, the teacher appears." I'm trying to pay attention to the tiny little miracles that appear every day that may seem like coincidence but are really serendipity, which is described in the Webster's dictionary as "linking together apparently innocuous facts to come to a valuable conclusion". It's like one thing leads to another, and by following the path, you will learn something valuable or something unexpected will happen.

The valuable and unexpected thing that has happened to me in the course of my therapy is a 180-degree turn from debilitating depression to excitement and optimism about sharing my writings with as many people as possible and continuing on my journey of discovering my true self, the one who pays no attention at all to my disability. My true self may live in a rickety house that needs a lot of work, yet it continues to learn and grow and strives to reach further than I ever thought possible. Damn fucking straight!

31

I Got Those
Staying-in-the-Hospital Blues

Okay, so here's how it went down. It was a Friday evening, March 16, 2004, at the end of another work week, TGIF. I was walking to my car slowly, using my walker on the very rickety cobblestone sidewalk in front of our work building. Mike, one of the salesmen, called over to me, "Bye, Renae, have a good weekend!" As I turned back toward him to say good night, my leg twisted and snapped my ankle in three different places. Down I went, smack down onto the sidewalk. Mike said he heard the bones breaking from where he was, which was at least forty feet away.

Apparently, Mike did not handle stressful situations very well. He ran over to me very shaken, because I was crying—I knew I was in big trouble. The other shoe had finally dropped. He repeatedly asked me, "What should I do?" And he was on the verge of panic himself. I blubbered between gasps to go and get some help, and he did. About eight or nine people came running out all trying to evaluate the situation and decide what the hell to do with me, a sobbing and blubbering mess of flesh crumpled on the sidewalk. They tried to stand me up, but it was apparent to them that my ankle was broken. They then decided I should be taken to a hospital. Someone gave me my purse so I could get my cell phone and call Lara and Brian.

A couple of guys carried me to Jason's car, and he and his fiancée, whom I had never met before and who seemed a little bit put out that they were the ones who got stuck taking me to the hospital and she had to sit in the backseat while I took her spot in the front next to her honey, did finally get me to the emergency room where Lara and Brian were waiting for me.

Luckily, the emergency room wasn't too busy that evening, so the orthopedic surgeon, Dr. Benbow, came out to speak to me and advised me that I was going to have to go straight into surgery. I was given some heavy-duty intravenous pain medication right there, which took effect immediately. Apparently, I was talking a little crazy to Lara and Brian because they were both laughing as I was being wheeled away. Those meds were awesome. I don't remember what they were, but I sure would like to have some of those on hand for when I just need a little vacation from my real life. By then, I had no idea what was going on.

After I woke up, I found out that I had a steel rod in my leg and a lot of staples to hold me together. I spent the next two months in the hospital's physical rehab facilities trying to get strong again. I've been in a wheelchair ever since not being able to gain enough strength to become ambulatory again. Goddam son of a bitch.

Okay . . . so that's the preliminary, and that's all you need to know for now, except that my orthopedic surgeon, Dr.

Benbow, was extremely handsome I didn't really mind when he came around to check up on me every now and then. And he was a really nice guy and not like one of those fucking arrogant bastards who act like you are really stupid and really don't deserve to be treated civilly or with compassion because we, as the patient and they as the gods are so far below them. God knows I've had plenty of those in my years on this earth.

God bless them both, Lara and Brian came to see me every day and most days twice—once in the morning before they went to work and again in the evening after work. They would bring me snacks and goodies and Starbucks coffee. The hospital food was really very good. I had a beautiful fruit salad with cottage cheese for lunch every day and something really nice in the evening including Chick-fil-A chicken wraps, which I love. Lara and Brian cheered me up when I was feeling down, helped to make me comfortable, and made fun of me in inappropriate ways—they just came to help me in any way they could. Lara in particular was my patient advocate, and she went to the once-a-week meeting for patient relatives to ask questions and get as much information as possible. You can't ever know what that means until you're in the situation where you can only get by with a little help from your friends. And I love them.

The only room that was available when I first went into the hospital had a shared bathroom. Yeesch! The guy in the next room kept trying to break out of the hospital, so I was a little on edge always thinking he was going to try to get into my room and get out of there that way. Of course, the bathroom has locks on both doors, so we both couldn't be in there at the same time, thank God for small favors. Plus,

I always heard him moaning and groaning while he was trying to poop, and that was just really yucky. He was always in there so long that when I needed to go to the bathroom, I had to wait a good long while until he was finished. Then I had to call a nurse's aide or a nurse to help me out of my bed and onto my wheelchair and then into the tiny bathroom and figure out ways to get onto the toilet.

The hospital bathrooms are not wheelchair friendly, even in the rehab section, so that made the hospital stay even more difficult. And then I had to do the whole thing in reverse again to get off the toilet onto my wheelchair and back into bed. I wasn't always a happy camper. And many times, I was a camper whose clothes were soaked with urine and filthy with poop because they gave us some kind of yucky drink to try to keep our bowels moving regularly. When you gotta go, you gotta go, and when the other guy was in there and then I had to wait for an aide and then we had to maneuver into the bathroom, it was sometimes too late to make it in time, and then there was always a lot of cleanup to do.

Being in the hospital is a very humbling experience, one where you have to throw your ego away. You are in need of much help, and humiliation and embarrassment are lingering near you at every moment ready to jump in and take part in whatever is going on around you. They're your constant companions, and they won't give up their post very easily. Little by little, I learned to keep them at bay, but still, they were with me, ready to pounce if they saw an opening. Humiliation and embarrassment are a couple of real mean fuckers, and I worked very hard every day to be cognizant of them so when I recognized their appearance I could push them out of my mind and replace them with my mantras, so it got easier and easier to handle any situation with at least a shred of dignity.

After a couple of days of complaining about my room, I was finally moved to an available private room with my very own bathroom. Somehow, when they bundled up the laundry in my old room, they also bundled up my cell phone, so I had to put in a lost-item report and cancel the phone account. A pain in the ass was what that was.

Rehab was tough going, and they were not about to let me out until I met the standards that they had set down to feel relatively sure I would be okay when I got home. I had to put in a couple extra weeks to get there, so I got to know the nurses and the aides pretty well. One of the nurses in particular seemed very harsh and snippy to me when I first met her. And then one day, she came in and was really very nice and helpful, so I said something to her like, "Wow, I really thought you were a nasty bitch, but I guess maybe you were just having a bad day." And she laughed and said she was sorry, but they were so shorthanded for a couple of days and she was just really tired and rushed.

So as she was leaving my room, I called her a fucking bitch, and she called me a goddamn idiot; from then on, we got along great. One day, I happened to have the wedding of Prince Charles and his longtime lover, Camilla, on the TV when she came in to give me my pills. Well, the opening ceremonies went on for so long, she asked me to call her when the wedding was about to start, which I did. We watched the royal wedding together, and if you happened to see it, I am sure you will have to agree Camilla's wedding dress and that thing that she wore on her head were really and truly ugly! Right? All the money in the world to get a brilliant designer and she decided to wear *that*! Anyway, we had a great time watching the whole royal family in all of their finery doing what the royals do best: being royal.

After about three weeks in the hospital, I started getting help from a new aide. He was a big, black Haitian man. He was really very kind and caring and very strong. The only time I was really uncomfortable with him was when I needed to go to the bathroom, and he came in to help me. He had to lift me off my bed, transfer me to the wheelchair and then into the tiny bathroom, and get me onto the toilet. I was in a skimpy hospital gown and had a cast on my leg. I was in pain, and he just picked me up and put me onto the toilet while I tried to keep my breasts and pubic area covered and still keep a shred of dignity. It didn't work. The weirdest part was he just kept standing there until I finally asked him to please close the door. I told him I would ring the bell when I needed help getting back into bed.

It seemed that now he was coming more and more regularly as my aide because we were never supposed to transfer alone. It was the hospital's policy to send female aides unless no one else was available. And it was getting uncomfortable to have a man help me with such intimate things, but still, I told myself he was acting professionally.

One day, about two or three o'clock in the morning, I woke up to some noise. I'm a very light sleeper, and I saw a strange man open my door and come into my room. As he was walking slowly toward me, he had his penis sticking out of his hospital gown and was peeing all over the floor and on my walker. He finally turned and made it to my sink, which was about five feet from my bed; he still had a good flow going. I was really afraid he was going to come over to my bed and pee on me, but he just stayed where he was. I pushed the button to call for help and told them there was a strange man in my room peeing in my sink. He just lifted up his hospital gown and had a strong, steady flow going, all the while making very noisy moaning and groaning sounds as if he was having an orgasm. That's just how good it felt for him to piss in my room.

Finally, four or five people came in, turned on the light, found him whizzing away, turned him around, and took him away still in the throes of ecstasy. Quite some time later, a cleaning lady came in. She mopped the floors and cleaned the stinky urine off of everything including my walker. I doubt if they got everything sanitized, but I guess I'll never know. It really surprised me when no one bothered to ask me if I was okay, which I was, but still, that would have been the polite thing to do and the professional thing for Christ's sake, me being a patient in their hospital and having just had a traumatic experience with someone who obviously should have been on the top floor in the psych ward.

It was explained to me later that the guy had been sleep walking, or rather piss walking, and that I didn't have to worry anymore because he was being restrained at night from now on. I had hoped that he would be stun-gunned and shackled and have a tattoo burned onto his forehead that said "Sink Pisser." But no such luck. I still saw him every day during physical therapy sessions. He never spoke to me and acted as though he didn't even see me. I doubt if he even remembered the incident. Thank God. And life went on.

One morning, Haitian guy came in to help me, and there I was sitting on the bed drenched in urine and diarrhea, humiliated beyond belief and crying hysterically. He kept reassuring me, telling me not to worry, he was there to help. After he cleaned up the whole friggin' mess and changed my sheets and everything, he just sat right beside me on a chair and put his hand across my chest and neck, and it occurred to me he could just strangle me right there and then. Now mind you, the door was closed and I was all alone with him. He started to stroke my hair with his other hand, all the while telling me everything was okay, he would take care of me, and I was so beautiful. I said, "Thank you," and that I just needed to sleep. He told me again not to worry, that he would be there to take care of me, and then he left. I didn't tell anyone for almost three days getting more and more upset, and in the meantime, I saw him around, and he was still coming in to help me and still being inappropriately friendly, touching me and telling me how pretty I was and how beautiful and soft my skin was. I was feeling increasingly helpless.

Here again, I found myself in a situation where I thought no one would believe me. I finally broke down sobbing and told Brian what had happened and how scared I was of the Haitian guy. Brian immediately called the head nurse, who came into the room right away. I explained what the big Haitian man had done. She was horrified and called two big shots from the hospital administration office, and they took a very detailed and formal complaint. They told me he had been at the hospital for only three months and had had no other complaints about him, but they would keep a close eye on him. They were there for a long time, and Brian stayed there with me, bless his goofy little heart. They asked me if I wanted to speak to the hospital's patient psychiatrist, and I said I did.

The next morning, the psychiatrist came in to speak to me. I told her all of the creepy things that had happened in the hospital, including the escapee sharing a bathroom with me, my cell phone lost in the laundry, the sink pisser, and the big Haitian guy getting a little too frisky. She asked if I had had other incidences in my life that were similar to the one with the big, black Haitian. And I explained a little about my past experiences with a couple of wankers who had crossed my path. She was very serious, caring, and validating. She advised that I get counseling when I got out of the hospital, which I did and still am doing.

I am sure that the big, black Haitian man had done this before. Women in a vulnerable position are afraid to speak up because there might be even worse repercussions. It took me three fucking days for God's sake. I mean what the hell!

I hope he gets caught in the act of inappropriate sexual behavior with a patient, and instead of calling the police, a few of the female aides—they look like a tough bunch, who might have a few issues with men themselves—take him "out back" with many shiny vials filled with assorted colored liquids and steel syringes and surgical instruments. I hope they inject him with behavior-modification drugs that change his inappropriate and naughty ways and just to make sure, they also inject him with huge doses of female hormones. Then to top it off, I hope they get the big medical procedure book, turn to page 685 with detailed, step-by-step pictures, and castrate him. And when he wakes up and asks them, "Why? Why did you do this to me?" they tell him, "Because you have been such a very, very bad man."

Eventually, he will be able to be employed in the transvestite entertainment circles. Big, black Haitian woman.

That'll teach him to touch and talk inappropriately to vulnerable, innocent female patients who need help in the hospital and not a big, black Haitian man to sexually harass and scare the shit out of them.

I've said it before, and I'll say it here again. I don't care what color you are, what nationality you are, what sexual orientation you are, what sex you are, or what religion you are as long as you just do your goddamn fucking job. Is that too much to ask? And do it with a smile and with professionalism. Fuck!

32

IMPURE THOUGHTS AND IMPURE DEEDS

Growing up Catholic and putting the fear of God and going to hell and burning up in flames for eternity with no relief to ever come; not even a sip of water or a hand-held fan; was terrifying, certainly to a young child and then continuing all the way into adulthood. Oh my God! Catholicism is the religion king when it comes to inducing guilt.

Religious pictures showing the devil amidst the flames of hell were there, hung on our neighbor's living room wall and in the catechism books we learned from in religion class every Wednesday. It was a constant reminder and a dreadful threat to the church faithful about our certain fate if we should stray from the path of the 10 Commandments. Only if you made it to confession in time to repent and suffer the punishment of ten Hail Mary's and five Our Fathers or whatever the priest deemed appropriate for whatever sins you actually confessed to or however long it had been since your last confession; only then could you start fresh and perhaps be saved from the everlasting inferno of hell.

Looking back on it now it seems so ridiculous but it is sure a goddamned good way to scare the shit out of innocent children and quivering adults to indoctrinate and enforce those beliefs. Behave yourself or you will go to hell. I was never really sure where the cutoff line was between going to Heaven to going to hell but I do know that I always confessed to having impure thoughts, doing impure deeds, and not honoring my father or my mother just to make sure. My confessions were always the same no matter what sins against the church I had committed.

I remember going into the confessional before Mass on Sundays knowing that everyone in the church was watching me and knowing that I was a bad little girl and knowing that the priest behind the black veil that separated the holy from the unholy knew good and goddamn fucking well who was kneeling on the other side even though he couldn't see who it was. And there were times when I was sure I was on the road to hell. I was toast.

It took many years of thinking and pondering, a lot of spiritual study and reading and a lot of soul-searching to slough off the beliefs that did not fit me and to identify and infuse those that rang true into the depths of my being. I no longer fear death. I now see the death of our human bodily form as the passing of another lifetime and still our true being, our true spirit, the true essence of who we really are lives on and can never be destroyed. How can the soul be obliterated?

I have looked into many religions and have passed on all organized religions because I see them as dividing people instead of bringing them together, as claiming to have the only one true God when in fact there is only one God with many different names and God is within all of us. I see organized religions using fear to gather and to keep their followers. I see organized religions taking money from their constituents and using it for selfish purposes and egotistical purposes to show that their church is better than others.

And the worst of all is all of the war and death and torture that has been brought throughout the ages and that have been done in the name of religion and continue to this day.

The paths that I have taken and the choices that I have made in my life have all led me to my here and now, making me the deeply spiritual person that I have become. I see life differently now. People and circumstances and objects and books come to me at the right time in order to enhance and nurture my being. Or so it seems.

I make no judgment about the choice that others make concerning their own spiritual beliefs. I believe that everyone learns and grows at their own pace and in their own fashion and none of us are here to judge anyone else's religious or spiritual beliefs no matter how differently they swerve from our own. Unless, of course it involves human sacrifice, slaughtering all of a particular race, or using God as your own personal spokesman to control the world. Hitler and Stalin are just two of many examples. Oh yes, and lest I forget there is Pol Pot another really fucking bad guy.

To judge another is the work and goal of the ego in order to make oneself feel better and the ego is never what we really are, it is not our inner self or our true being that will last for eternity.

And so my path lately is taking the form of realizing when my ego is getting in the way and for at least a little while living in the here and now, not worrying about the future or fretting about what was done in the past. I make it a practice to do this every night before I go to sleep and I have found that I sleep much better when I give all my problems and thoughts and worries up to the universe to handle and I can let my body rest and heal.

And the good thing is that no matter what impure thoughts I have or impure deeds I am guilty of, I am good and goddamn positive I am not going to fucking hell.

33

FLACCID PUSSY

Just about the most gut-wrenching thing Fuckwad ever said to me in his long list of checks in the minus column of my personal traits was that he couldn't even feel anything anymore when we had sex because my pussy was so loose and flaccid. He had never complained about that before; we had always had a great sex life until my MS started to worsen. When he told me that, my world crumbled beneath me. I fell apart. He told me no one would ever want me what with the flabby pussy and all. So with those few sentences, he even took away my ability to think of myself as a sexual woman—a pretty, perky, desirable woman. I was now reduced to a body part not usually talked about in polite company. And that certainly was not a polite thing to say.

Words are mightier than the sword, and they can cut out pieces of our self, chunk by chunk, until there is hardly anything left and very little reserve to heal the wounds and become whole again. I changed that day. I changed in how I saw myself, felt about myself, and presented myself. I went from a successful businesswoman, who loved to flirt and look pretty, to a flaccid-pussied leech, a bloodsucking cunt who would never again satisfy a man, who walked like an old woman, and who was just plain pathetic.

It's hard to bounce back from that when you have so consistently woken up every day to one cruel scolding about one thing or another.

I had no reply. The sword had cut out my tongue, and I had no words to fight with.

Divorce was next on the agenda. I had finally reconciled myself to the fact that he was already gone. I had prayed many nights while crying myself to sleep, begging God to give me the strength not to love him anymore. It was easier just to relent; I had no strength to fight, and I was sick.

Fuckwad found a divorce lawyer, and we agreed to divorce amicably and not to put our ten-year-old son into the hell of having to choose sides between his mommy and daddy. We signed the divorce papers: irreconcilable differences. Well, I should say so! Even though his cock was enormous, a whopping six and a half inches long, my pussy was just too stretched out and flaccid for him to feel his dick inside of me. Again, some comebacks are just too late—this one, actually about eleven and half years too late. I should have said to him that his dick was so small that I couldn't feel anything from his tiny little pee-pee. I thought of it in Dr. Cinzia's office, wouldn't you know.

It took all the nerve I could muster, but I had to know if it was true. Was my pussy really that unsatisfactory? I started to flirt online. I put up a profile on AOL for a forty-four-year-old divorced woman looking for a man in the thirty-five to forty-five age range. I have always been attracted to younger men. I got lots of replies because my ad was very funny and different, and it went something like this:

Are you schizophrenic, delusional, have any STDs? Are you kind to children and animals? Do you use steroids? Are you narcissistic? Do you have a dual personality, a driver's license, a toupee? Do you cheat on women? Are you a priest looking for a good time? Do you have delusions of grandeur, think you are God's gift to women, or have acid reflux, acne, ulcers, hammertoe, athlete's foot, alcoholism, gambling or sexual addiction, or small feet? Do you chew your fingernails? Have you ever been in prison and why? Do you have a sense of humor, collect art glass, or have a dog, hemorrhoids, or halitosis? Do you take antidepressants or illegal drugs? Do you see a psychiatrist or go to therapy? Are you bald, or do you have hair plugs? Do you dye your hair? Are you a vegetarian or a carnivore? Have dandruff, claustrophobia, obesity, a bad back, or eczema? Do you take female hormones or Viagra? Are you a mass murderer, a stalker, a pedophile (I believe this is why so many states have a death penalty law), a con artist, or a writer of bad checks? Do you have scabies, goiters, or impetigo? Have you ever had a sex change, and do you have a job? And most important, do you crack your toes and do you have a grand sense of humor? E-mail back and let me know because that will give us something to talk about. And please be honest.

Most of the replies held no interest for me and were just basically very bland. I was looking for someone who would "get it." Some of them did, and I would call them up and talk to them to see if anything clicked. One guy was very persistent, but he was so shkeevy and sent a picture of himself posing in skin tight, red underwear as though I would find something like this attractive. He kept e-mailing me and being basically a pest, so I finally put him on my do-not-accept list. If you have to flaunt it, you just ain't got it. Some of them just wanted a free sex line and wanted me to talk dirty to them. If I was going to do that, then I most certainly was going to be paid and paid well. Looking back on it now, it doesn't seem like such a bad idea; I certainly could have used the money, but at that point in time, I had more important things on my mind, such as figuring out how I was going to live another day, finding guys I could talk dirty to in person, and not being used by the guys who wouldn't have to pay somebody to talk dirty to them while they masturbated.

Shitheads!

When Fuckwad took Ryan to Dallas to see how it would go with his "new family," I slept with lots of strange men and put myself in dangerous situations. I made a lot of men very happy, and not one of them complained about my pussy. It felt great to feel like a woman, to have power, to feel desirable and wanted, and to be complimented. I always used protection. I was looking for something that I had lost. I admit that I went about it in a way that put my children's mother at risk, and for that, I am sorry.

I met most of the men first in public places, in the local diner or bookstores. With some of them, however, I went to their apartments, not knowing exactly who or what I was meeting. I had communicated with all of them via Internet and /or telephone, but people lie to make themselves seem attractive. I was willing to take that risk to validate myself and prove that despite all of my obvious and not-so-obvious flaws, I was still a woman to be admired and deserved to be treated well. I just couldn't bear to sit home all alone thinking about Fuckwad with our little boy meeting his mistress and her family. Instead, I took it as an opportunity to fortify myself and start to live on my own.

I am not sorry, however, that for a short time I was a slut. No way around it, my dear children, your mama was a hussy. I needed to regain my independence, my power as a woman. I needed to not let men take advantage of me; rather I took advantage of them and gave them a good time in return, so that neither of us was hurt. We both gained another good life experience. Many of them wanted to see me again, but I did not want to see them, which fortified me and helped me to regain my strength and power as a woman, with or without MS, because even then I was walking with a cane, stumbling and fumbling and struggling. Yet these men that I had seduced saw past my physical weaknesses.

And when the sex was done, we spent hours talking about our lives. I again began to see myself as an accomplished and interesting woman who helped start and run several businesses, and I saw that I was no dummy. A slut, yes . . . but not a dumb one.

And then it came time to drag my flabby, flaccid pussy to Dallas on that goddamned fucking bus, twenty-one hours with all the symptoms of MS, scared silly, and yet in a strange way, with the calmness of knowing that I would be okay; that the universe had led me there for a reason; that I was being taken on a path to something bigger, something larger and beyond knowing; and that if I paid attention to the clues around me and opened my eyes and my whole being to any and all possibilities, I could find inner peace—and a new life.

It has taken me many, many years to get to the place where I am now, with over a year and a half spent with Dr. Cinzia in weekly therapy sessions with her untold wealth of information and suggestions, her understanding and empathy, and, of course, her appreciation of my sense of humor, which seems to match hers; I still rise steadily forth, and little by little, I am finding that peace toward which I strive.

So here I am today, starting to feel more alive and getting stronger inside if not out. I really would like to find a wonderful man with a nine-inch penis to fill up my normal-sized pussy and stay with me through thick and thin, till death do us part—preferably from old age lying next to each other while we peacefully cross over in our sleep and not from murder or mayhem. Perhaps we could lovingly hold hands while we drink hemlock-laced Kool-Aid or green tea.

34

FINALLY, AN AIDE WHO IS AFRAID OF GOD!

After two months of waiting patiently to be appointed yet another home health aide, I received a call from an agency that I had chosen. The first thing that I did, was to go to our social services website for disabled and aged people and check and see what sort of ratings or what sort of naughtiness and abuses were reported about them. I finally found one that looked pretty good. The next thing was to ask the questions that I had previously printed out to ask the agency since I have had a god-awful time in the past getting an agency and an aide who would not try to manipulate me, take advantage of me, abuse our social services system or me in any manner, or to see just how far they could push the envelope before I just had enough and fired their lazy, manipulative, creepy asses.

I have learned much along the way in the therapy I attend with my dear Dr. Cinzia about how to set boundaries, and how not to be taken advantage of so I was very curious to see what sort of critter was going to come crawling through my door.

To say that I was cautious considering the past history of the aides that had been taking care of me is an understatement. So I had made a list of things that I had expected her to do within the hours that I was entitled to and I took her on a tour of the kitchen and the rest of my living area, showing her what to do and how to do it. Now, as it turns out she is from Ethiopia, looks to be in her early to mid 40s, is very gentle and caring and is able to lift me safely in and out at the shower which had been such a traumatic experience with all of the other aides I have had before. She has now been my caretaker for three weeks and she is doing a damn good job. She asked me intermittently if I like her and I always say yes I like her very much and she says I love you and I will treat your home as if it were my own.

Amazingly, Aster, that is her name, which in Ethiopian means a star, will do all sorts of tasks that I ask her to do that all of my other aides have balked at, many times because they were not physically able to bend or are just too lazy or just really didn't give a shit. Astor is doing everything I ask her to do, willingly, and always with a smile. When I ask her to do something that I think might be a little over the line she just reassures me and says that's my job. I am here to help you. And so it is done.

The thing that makes me a little squeamish is when she starts to tell me about her sick father in Ethiopia and how long it's been since she has seen him and the cost of the plane flights to get there and yet I try to show empathy and don't ask for any further information. I have heard horror stories of home health aides taking advantage of the people in their care manipulating them to give them vacation, cars, groceries, pay their rent and expenses etc. etc. and it breaks my heart. So as soon as I hear even a hint of Aster's story I immediately turn the attention to something else such as putting antibiotic cream on a large bandage and sticking it to the pressure sore on my ass. That usually does the trick to bring things back into focus.

There is one thing that really and truly impresses me about Aster. It is something that I should put on my list of qualifications for any aides that I may need in the future. It is the one thing that has given me trust in her, relaxes me so if I am doing something else while she is in another room I am confident that she is not snooping or stealing or opening and closing drawers that I have personal things in, such as money, medications, and my vibrator.

So anyway, the thing that has gotten me to trust her so implicitly up to this point is that she is afraid of God. She feels that God is watching her and sees everything that she does and if she even thinks about doing anything wrong God will smite her and she will suffer the flames of hell for all eternity. Isn't that just awesome?! I mean really, what better deterrent could there be than an angry Almighty paying very close attention to every little thing you do? Am I wrong to take pleasure in this? I am just going to enjoy it for a while and see where it leads.

Now when she first told me this I was so taken aback I tried to assure her that God is good and God is forgiving but she would have none of it and then I just thought to myself, don't try to persuade her in any way or fashion because this is actually a very good thing. I have Aster for a very short time and I know very little about her but I know she has the fear of God in her heart, that she is Christian, and perhaps somewhere along the line there has been a miscommunication and misunderstanding in the workings of a Christian God or perhaps and more than likely, she just may not be as spiritually advanced to the stage of living a life of goodness just for the sake of goodness and not being good for the fear of consequences by a big bad God.

At any rate, I see this working to my advantage and we are getting along very, very well. I'm confident that this will continue and that Astor will be with me for long time to come.

Don't worry, I'm not going to actually try to put anymore fear of God into her because my belief system is so different from hers and yet I do believe that we all advance spiritually at our own pace and it is not my job to convince her that she is just being plain silly nor her job to convince me to read the Bible every day. Firstly, because it could just come and bite me in the ass. Secondly, because I am keeping to a professional relationship where Astor is here to help me; that is her job. And so right now I am just being very grateful to the universe for sending her to me and to Astor's big bad God for keeping her on the straight and narrow. As she says over and over, "thank you God, thank you God." as she presses her hands together and bows.

35

JOE, JAKE, AND JUXTAPOSITION

It's no secret that dogs love stinky things; the stinkier the better so it should have come as no surprise when we found out that our French Bulldog, Joe, is really attracted to my catheter supplies. He especially loves to chew on the hard plastic parts that connect the hose to the urine collecting container and I have spent a lot of time, money, and angst having to deal with the consequences of this very disgusting, pissy ritual. He just sees it as one great stinky chew toy and to add to that, if there is any overflow from the container he will lick it up as though it were a special treat that I have left just for him.

I know this is just so god-awful to even be reading about but imagine finding this chew toy all gnarled and twisted and marked with dog teeth just when you are getting ready for bed and just imagine that you don't have any backup because you have used them all up in his previous catheter chewing episodes which, by the way, he does on the sly because he knows that that particular item is off-limits; and yet he just can't seem to contain himself. I try to remember to make sure that I have put everything in a bucket just for that purpose of keeping it off of the floor but sometimes I forget and then there is hell to pay. My bad. He is slowly learning to leave it alone but it's been a long hard battle that has included crazy glue, duct tape, and rubber bands to try and mend the incidences one at a time. I mean I use those things on the catheter connectors and hoses, not on Joe, the dog, although I've been tempted.

There have been many times when the catheters have leaked or come apart and I have woken up with soaking wet sheets. I've cried with frustration from having to change and wash my clothes and bedding and I can't blame it all on Joe's catheter fetish; some of it was just on the learning curve, some just because of ignorance, and some from exhaustion.

I still love Joe no matter what mischief he gets into. He's just doing the best he knows how and "when he knows better he does better" to quote one of my favorite authors, Maya Angelou. It's just one more of the cluster fucks that I have had to conquer.

When Ryan, my son, was just a little guy, probably when he was seven or eight, he went to the pet store with his dad and came back with a Burmese-Python. That's right a snake that he named Jake. He got all the equipment for Jake and got him all set up nice and cozy although there is nothing cozy about a snake. Interesting to watch but not too interested in the snuggling. If I'm going to have a pet it sure as hell better be interested in snuggling! Once a week he would be fed a live mouse which he would stalk and then strike, open his jaws really, really wide and slowly and methodically eat the whole thing in one sitting and you could see the shape of the mouse as his muscles slowly contracted and the little critter went into his body. It was a wonderful treat for him, just not so wonderful for the mouse. Mother Nature in all her gory splendor. Often times he would be left out of the cage and liked to be on people because snakes are cold-blooded and enjoy the warmth of people and he spent a lot of time around Ryan's neck. So anyway Jake became part of our family.

There were times when Jake went missing and we would have to hunt for him but we always found him under the couch or behind dresser. And then there was one time when he went missing for over two weeks and we couldn't find him anywhere even after we searched every nook and cranny we could think of. He went missing just before Christmas and after all the holidays were over and I was taking the decorations off of the Christmas tree I gasped in surprise because there was Jake curled up at the very top of the Christmas tree enjoying the warmth of the lights.

He actually scared the shit out of me but after I collected myself for a bit, I yelled for Ryan to come over because I was a little shkeeved and shocked about finding him up there. Ryan was so thrilled to have Jake the Snake back once again as he uncoiled him from the tree and put him back in his nice warm aquarium. To be truly honest with you I wasn't all that happy to see him again and I was a little disgruntled to find him in the tree. But oh, the agonizing sacrifices we make for our children.

Quite sometime later Ryan and I had been out someplace shopping and Jake had been left out of his cage. Thinking nothing of it, because it was just a normal thing, we went into the kitchen to put the bags down and as I put one small paper bag down on the floor, out of nowhere Jake lunged at me and bit my hand in that fleshy inside part right below my thumb and he would not let go. I was screaming and thrashing my arm frantically up and down over and over with the Python still attached to me, Jake flapping as a 2 foot long extension of my arm, I was trying desperately to get him off of me but he held on for dear life for a good long time until finally he let go and flew someplace in the kitchen. I was so horrified and disgusted I was shaking.

My hand started to swell up immediately and you could see the teeth marks as it started to turn purple where he was trying to swallow me whole as though I were a mouse, a really big mouse. Ryan was screaming, I was screaming; we could not believe what had just happened. He came from under the stove and apparently I had startled him with the bag or he saw the bag and thought there was a mouse in it or he just went stark raving mad and bit the hand that fed him. Well by now Ryan and I were scared shitless and we were afraid to go anywhere near that giant Burmese monster so we got the broom and staying as far away from him as possible, swept him into a small box and hurriedly and nervously put him back in his cage and put the top on and locked it.

Well as far as I was concerned, that put the kibosh on any of the love that I really didn't have for him in the first place. Ryan on the other hand seemed to get over it pretty quickly (but, of course he wasn't the one who had a giant purple welt with visible teeth marks on his hand for three frickin' weeks) and so Jake was once again back in the fold. But oh, the agonizing sacrifices we make for our children.

Renae Clare

A few days ago I got a call from Ryan who is now grown and on his own and he told me something very interesting which I did not know could be done before. One of his cats, named Frankie Boy, has been given a sex change operation! I know, I know! Really amazing, right? Well it seems that Frankie Boy had a calcium buildup in his urine which was caused from eating the wrong kind of cat food. These sharp little calcium crystals have to pass through his penis and apparently cause discomfort if not god awful pain. After visiting the veterinarian's office a decision was made to turn his penis into a slit/vagina in order for his urine to pass more freely from his/her urethra which in the Webster's dictionary is defined as . . . the **urethra** (from Greek οὐρήθρα—*ourethra*) is a tube that connects the urinary bladder to the outside of the body. In males, the urethra travels through the penis and carries semen as well as urine. In females, the urethra is shorter and emerges above the vaginal opening . . . I find it astonishing how far modern medicine has come in the last decade. And that goes for pets as well as for humans. Sex change operations for animals; huh . . . who knew?

So now that that operation has been done Ryan has noticed a visible change, not only in the appearance of his/her genitals but also in her state of mind. In retrospect he has realized that since he was a kitten, Frankie Boy showed signs of not being comfortable in his own body. He always wanted to play with the girl kittens and loved it when someone would dress him up in frilly clothing. He had always been such a picky eater preferring the cat food that is served in crystal bowls and not the large economy size his masters always got cheaper at one of the superstores. And there were other subtle signs as well. For example he spent an extraordinary amount of time on his grooming and loved to try new fur styles using his own spit to create gorgeous coifs. Plus, he would save and gather up his hairballs and slowly and meticulously making incredible sculptures. Not fascinating to humans, but obviously fascinating to the other cats in the house because they would all stand around and look at these sculptures for a long time as though they were exhibits in a modern art museum.

And so now Ryan is thinking that in some unconscious way Frankie Boy had created his illness as an excuse to get the sex change operation he had been so longing for since he was just a little kit.

Now Ryan reports that Frankie Boy will not come to him or even acknowledge any of his family unless they call him; I mean her, Arethra Franklin or just Arethra. It seems it's been hard for everyone to adjust to the new name but now Arethra feels like the female cat she was always meant to be. And the best part is, she can finally pee with no pain and without having to look at that goddamn penis she knows was an aberration and was never meant to be there in the first place. You go girl!

36

MUSIC TO SOOTHE THE SAVAGE BEAST

There is a dreaded beast that lives just under the surface of my daughter's psyche like one of those prehistoric creatures we saw in the movie Jurassic Park. How cute and adorable and sweet she looks, and then out of the blue, she raises her wings, snarls at you with her razor-sharp teeth bared, and comes at you before you can even blink.

So I was sitting in Dr. Cinzia's waiting room, eyes closed, listening to the wonderful classical radio station that is always on when I come into her office. Then I heard an advertisement come on for the Dallas Symphony at the Meyerson Philharmonic Center. In a voice that could melt glaciers, the male announcer told us that for three days only, starting the following day, they would be playing Ravel's Boléro as well as other musical pieces. Since Boléro is my favorite classical music piece ever, I decided then and there to call as soon as I got home and make arrangements for the matinee on Sunday. The theater has special seating for gimps like me in wheelchairs as well as the tottering elderly and people with canes, walkers, and various other devices, who cannot maneuver stairs—seats that are so wonderful because they have a really great view (and we know exactly where we're going to be sitting whenever we go there) in that wonderful section made especially for those of us who are feeble in body but not in mind.

When I told Lara about the plans I had made, I told her that we needed to do something to get out of the slump that we were so deeply embedded in, and we were going to do something fun and adventurous. She was so excited! It felt so good to, for once, be the bearer of good news.

Sunday came, and the Handi-ride bus got us there with time to spare, lickety-split, no worrying about where to park or how to get there or how to maneuver my rickety body in and out of the car and from one place to another. We got there so quickly we even had an hour and a half to dawdle and have brunch with the various college deans and heart surgeons and other uppity-ups and cultural ones, and we felt right at home among them.

We found our way to our seats, having been led there by one of the staff. She took away one of the regular chairs in order to accommodate my wheelchair. And there we sat amidst our fellow feeble patrons, enjoying the people-watching. We felt the growing excitement as the theater seats filled up and the orchestra started to practice. Lara noticed a woman with a large fur hat, whom we had seen at lunch, down in the first row. You couldn't miss her, which I'm sure was her intention. The concert was amazing; Boléro was the finale. It was a standing ovation for most people; I was standing with them in my heart.

During the concert, Lara nudged me and whispered for me to look at the elderly couple beside her who were holding hands and keeping time with the music as one. It just goes to show you once again that love has no boundaries and music is a language in and of itself. It was so sweet and touching. I think Boléro was their favorite too.

We got home, so happy that we had done something together that was so extraordinary. In just that one action, we had gone from adversaries to friends and comrades, and the amazing thing is that we have stayed that way. We haven't backtracked, and it has made all the difference in the world to my mind-set, my level of strength, and my ability to do many more things on my own. It is amazing when you realize just how much energy it takes to live on the negative side. And life is a lot more fun when you just make up your mind to put all your negative thoughts and reasons not to do something interesting, exciting, and fun away and just do it, come what may.

The next day, Lara came to me and gave me a big, long hug and lots of kisses. She thanked me so much for making all the arrangements and told me what a wonderful time she had had. We agreed that we would never fall back into that awful negative rut again. The music really did soothe the savage beast, and ever since then, her wings have been hidden and her teeth are back to normal, and she doesn't snarl nearly as much. She's been helpful and caring and respectful, and our wild and wicked senses of humor are back in full force. I really think that we took a 180-degree turn.

That beast has been soothed at least for the time being, and we have plans to see Mannheim Steamroller at the Meyerson Theatre for their wonderful Christmas program, which will feature our favorite Christmas songs, including

"Choral of the Bells" and "Little Drummer Boy." Another exciting adventure awaits us.

Now that I think of it, many interesting and wonderful things have happened just from my having been in Dr. Cinzia's waiting room. Sometimes, I am early and meet another patient or someone waiting for a patient there in her office. I often learn valuable information from them, so I am sure it is the place I am meant to be. And I am sure that the universe is telling me that I am in the right place and the therapy is not just in the doctor's office but everywhere. It is writing about whatever is on my mind or has been assigned to me by Dr. Cinzia; it is getting ready to go, which takes a lot of forethought and preparation; it is everything from the bus trip to the people who have helped me on the elevators and helped me get through doors and the people who were concerned about me when my bus was late. It is especially in her waiting room where there is quiet and time just to be.

And there is always music there to soothe the savage beasts who are brave enough to find out what is holding them back and to connect the dots to see how their past has led them to their now.

And please note, I did not curse one fucking time during this whole fucking story.

37

LIPSTICK FETISH

Before my long and torturous journey to Texas, I did tons of research on the Internet about resources for people with MS and for people with disabilities. One thing I found out was that Texas was at the bottom of the list for services for disabled people. In between trying to find men to validate my womanhood in New York, which in actuality can be interpreted as men to fuck and help me prove to myself that my pussy really wasn't that flaccid, I was really a very good lover in spite of having MS, and I was still desirable, interesting, and worthy.

I spent a lot of time on the computer trying to find interesting men who lived in the Dallas area. I did not want to feel all alone without a friend or companion or someone to help me muddle through the hell I was experiencing. I connected with a couple of people/men whom I found interesting and with whom I found a connection. After speaking on the Internet for several months, we spoke on the phone.

The one guy I liked the best actually met and fell in love with someone before I ever got to meet him. Too fuckin' bad. But life is taking me on a journey and I am just traveling the dirt paths wherever they may lead. And I have gotten to know intimately many cocks of all colors, shapes, sizes, lengths, and widths, including one that was so crooked that it took some maneuvering to get it in. But with a little persistence, it finally hit the spot.

And so it was time to say good-bye to choice number one and hello to choice number two.

As it turned out, his wife had died about a year and a half earlier and he had two kids; one was a married daughter, who was jealous of any woman who came near her dad, and the other was a son who lived with him because he had ADD and could not hold down a job. I did not find out any of this until I got to Texas. You never find out the negative stuff until you're right up front and close. This is the case with most pictures that people put up of themselves. His picture had been taken fifteen years earlier when he was fifty to sixty pounds lighter. Not a gray hair was visible in the picture. I actually posted a very current picture of myself, since at the time I was such a babe and there wasn't a wheelchair in sight. I used a cane and walked at a slant but you can't tell that by looking at a picture.

When I met him in person, I found out it was his ex-wife who had died and he was the one who actually took care of her while she was dying of cancer. He had lost his house and was now living in a double-wide trailer; he had lost his job because he elected to stay with her and also spent any savings that he had had. So he stayed with her literally until death did they part, and they weren't even married any longer. Even though I saw him for only about three months, he will forever have my respect for stepping up and being a real man. Last I heard of him, he was the food manager at one of the finer hotels in Dallas. I wish him all the best.

On a quirky little side note, Fuckwad's lover told him to let me know that I should be careful about dating someone who lives in a trailer park because all sorts of unsavory people apparently lived there. Lovely of them, don't you think, to be giving me fucking dating advice now that they could give a shit about my health or well-being? Fuckwad had even told me when I first started dating again after our divorce to make sure to get an AIDS test—and this from a man who could very easily have brought AIDS into my bed or even more succinctly, into my own flaccid pussy. What a fucking cocksucker! Piss Ant! Righteous Pool of Putrid Puke! Dick Weed! Asshole Motherfucking Shithead! Even as I was trying to move on with my life, he felt the need to keep me scared. Need I say more? And yes I did get an AIDS test, and yes, it was negative.

So now back to choice number two, I will call him the Snorer. I slept over at his house one time. His snoring was so loud I hardly got any sleep that night. I was honest with him about why I would not stay the night. You know how they say that when a tornado is approaching, it sounds like a freight train? Well, that is what it was like with the Snorer. He was a really sweet guy, a nice guy, a guy that someone was sure to fall in love with. But it wasn't gonna be me.

First things first, he couldn't get it up. I mean, eventually he did, but God, what a lot of work! Now, not to toot my own horn, but I give a mean blow job and as I came to find out, his ex-wife, while they were married, *never* blew him. So for him, I was a gift from heaven. Consider this:

you have come to the front door of the woman you have been getting to know for the past four months or so via e-mails, phone calls, and instant messages, etc. You ring the doorbell, and there she is, totally naked. She takes your hand, quickly closes the door, gives you a big hug and kiss, and then leads you directly to the bed where you lie down. She unzips your pants and takes them off along with your underwear and proceeds to give you the best blow job you have had . . . ever. There's nothing like a great blow job to make a man happy, especially if it is unexpected and from someone he's actually never met before. And he doesn't even have to pay for it! You guessed it; that was me at my sluttiest. Well . . . just about my sluttiest.

Now, please remember that this was my slutty period, like when Vincent van Gogh went through his blue period. Okay, so not the same thing, exactly, but you get the picture. I know that Vincent was schizophrenic and dealing with terrible demons.

I, in my own way, dealt with my demons by being a slut. My slutty period of time was short-lived and is long gone but certainly not forgotten. In retrospect, I don't regret any of it. I always had safe sex, and I met a lot of really interesting people. By then, I was in my mid-forties and had never had a slutty time before. The only two men I had slept with before this both eventually became my husbands. And now I know that I have a perfectly normal pussy—though now that I don't have a man in my life to do any pruning or landscaping for, the foliage is getting a little out of control. Nonetheless, I learned to be confident and free in my sexuality and in my womanhood with or without a man to validate me.

Now every relationship has its gives and takes, right? I did lots of nice things for the Snorer, and he did lots of nice things for me. At the time, he was working as a courier and I would go on rides with him. He would show me the city and take me places. He took me out to eat and to the movies and did all those sorts of normal things. I still did not have a job because I still had no car to get around.

It would be another three weeks before I finally got Fuckwad's 1988 Chevy Nova, which he didn't need anymore because he got a much nicer car. He needed a nice car so he could look like the successful, upstanding man about town that he wanted to portray himself to be. I just needed a shitty car to get me to the very first job I interviewed for, which I got and accepted immediately and gratefully. I stayed there for ten years until the other shoe finally dropped and I became paralyzed on my left side and wheelchair-bound—but that's neither here nor there. Back to the Snorer.

One thing that the Snorer loved to do for me was to take me shopping for lipstick—expensive lipstick—and he loved to help me pick out the color. Well, wasn't that nice of him? He would do this every couple of weeks. I never asked him for anything; he always did it out of the goodness of his heart and probably to keep those blow jobs coming. Eventually, I figured something out. He always liked me to wear lipstick when we had sex, and he loved to kiss me and get lipstick all over his mouth and his cock. One day, it hit me—not his cock, I mean the light bulb over my head: the Snorer had a lipstick fetish!

Not that I minded exactly, but I did find it peculiar. So one day, I asked him about it. He told me a story that certainly explained it all. His mother was an Avon lady, and she would have Avon parties at her house or other people's houses. She would take her little boy, the Snorer, who was then five or six years old and use him as a demonstrator for her lipsticks and makeup products. All the other women thought he was so cute and adorable because his mother kept his hair long and curly.

Everyone thought he made such a beautiful little girl. You think that doesn't fuck you up good for the rest of your life? He was lucky he only came out with a lipstick fetish. I wouldn't be surprised if he had a secret life as a transvestite. I do know that his poor dead ex-wife was a very tall and large woman and that he had never thrown away any of her clothing or the lavish jewelry she loved to wear. He still had drawers full of her makeup and lipstick.

When he told me the story, I actually started to cry, feeling such anguish for what that little guy had to go through and the lifelong effects that parents' perversions could have on their children. He told me he never said no to his mother because he just loved to please her. I guess he helped her to sell a lot of Avon products, thereby helping to support the family.

There was one thing that really upset me that the Snorer said to me. He said (and I quote): "If you had not breast-fed your kids for so long, maybe your boobs wouldn't be so saggy." I was so angry I could have spit a brick. As if he had any say about how I raised my children and what I did for them so that I could be more attractive to him! What gall!

There were so many things I could've said to him about his giant beer gut, his inability to get a decent erection, his wanker-ass lazy son, and his spoiled-rotten, vindictive, money-hungry daughter. But I held my tongue and didn't say anything bad about him or his children.

One thing I have learned along the way is not to say anything that you can't take back. It takes much more energy to explain away what you said than to walk away from the situation and give it some thought. I just told him that was a really nasty thing to say to me, grabbed my purse and my cane, left in a huff, stumbled to my car and drove home.

The Snorer's lipstick fetish was not what made me finally break up with him. It was his son, who was twenty-two at the time, slept on the couch even though he had his own room, couldn't keep a job because he was always late or didn't show up, and was a complete slob. The Snorer talked about his son all of the time, and it just was not a problem that I wanted to take on. The Snorer was a good man, but I did not love him and was certainly not ready to settle down with anyone since I was still in the process of working on Fuckwad. Even after twelve years, I'm still working on it.

So I broke it off and felt an immediate sense of relief. I actually did it over the telephone, not having the courage to do it face-to-face. He was pretty upset and asked me why. I told him truthfully that dealing with his son was too much for me to take on, and he said he understood and then asked if we could please just stay friends. I said no, that it just wouldn't work knowing that my MS was making me more and more exhausted and I had to prioritize where I spent my energy. It was the first time in my life I started to take care of me first. Notice I said "started to." I still had a very long way to go and still do, but at least now I am cognizant and paying attention to my actions. Along the way, I have collected some very pretty lipstick. I just don't have anyone's cock to leave it on.

38

TWENTY QUESTIONS I WOULD LIKE TO ASK DR. CINZIA

Of course, I'm not allowed to ask any of the following questions. Considering that Dr. Cinzia has so adamantly insisted I apply certain boundaries to my home health aides, I suppose those same boundaries must also apply to the therapist-patient relationship that I have with her. But goddamn it, I really, really want to know.

1. What does your husband do?

2. Why were you drawn to clinical psychology?

3. Did you have a happy childhood?

4. Are you happily married, and if so, for how long, how did you meet, and does your family like him?

5. What is the strangest case/patient that you have ever treated?

6. What kind of traumas have you experienced in your life to make you such a phenomenal therapist and so very wise?

7. Have you ever suffered from mental problems?

8. Am I your favorite patient?

9. If not, who is your favorite patient and what the hell is his or her problem?

10. Do you like treating men or women better?

11. What is the thing in your life that you are most sorry for?

12. Would you show me a picture of your husband?

13. Are your parents still alive, and if so, do you have a good relationship with them?

14. Do you have children?

15. Do you get along with the therapist who is your partner?

16. How many brothers and sisters do you have, and are you a close family?

17. What is the average time people spend in your care?

18. Tell me the truth, Dr. Cinzia, do you secretly talk to your husband about the crazy people that you treat every day?

19. Have you ever gotten really angry with a patient and stopped treating him/her because you just couldn't take it anymore?

20. Do you have any idea how much I admire and love you and how thankful I am that you have entered my life and changed it forever?

I have many more questions that I'd like answers for, but I'll just leave it at that for now. Besides, I know I'll never get the fucking answers to the ones I've already asked. Inquiring minds want to know, and I have a very fucking inquiring mind.

39

Suggested List of Questions to Ask Your Home Health Aide

Below is a list that I have created from my own personal experience. I have made mistakes too numerous to mention when dealing with home health aides and home health care agencies. Lucky you get to gain invaluable knowledge from my miseries.

- How long have you been working as an aide?

- How many clients do you currently care for?

- Are you strong enough and healthy enough to lift and transfer me safely?

- Do you have a car?

- Is there anything that you definitely will not do?

- Do you understand and speak English clearly?

- What kind of training have you had to become an aide?

- Have you ever been cited or reported for a wrongdoing either by a client or by your agency?

- Are you able to bend over to pick up objects that I drop?

- Will you need to go back to your country of origin in order to renew a visa?

- Have you recently taken a drug test?

- What hours can you work? Make sure he or she can work the hours that you need.

40

And Now a List of Questions I Would Really Like to Ask My Home Health Care Aide

This list is more extensive and will give much more in-depth insight into how you may feel as you come upon your own health care aides whether they care for you or your loved one at home, in a hospital, or in some other care facility. With this information you will be able to make more of an informed decision about who you let into your personal life. It is not unusual to go through five aides or more until you find someone you are comfortable with. It is your right to feel safe and well cared for. And don't ever be afraid or uncomfortable to ask questions. Learn to be a loud mouth if necessary and remember, "The squeaky wheel gets the worm" . . . no, no, no, the oil. "The squeaky wheel gets the oil."

- Do you have more than an eighth-grade education?

- Have you ever worked as an aide before?

- Am I your first client?

- Am I in danger when you try to lift and transfer me in and out of the shower chair, bed, or wheelchair?

- Do you have a car? If so, do you know how to drive it?

- Do you have a valid driver's license?

- Have you ever taken and failed a drug test?

- Do you have a huffy attitude?

- Do you understand fucking English?

- Have you had any kind of training to become an aide or are you just winging it?

- Have you ever been in prison? And for what crime?

- Are you an illegal alien?

- Have you ever been reported for mistreating, intimidating, or physically, mentally, psychologically, or sexually abusing a person in your care?

- Are you too overweight to bend over and pick up things that I drop?

- Will you need to go back to your country of origin in order to renew a visa? If so, would you be respectful enough to let me know before I hire you, so I can make an informed fucking decision?

- Would you call me and ask me if it is okay for you to bring your bratty spoiled child with you to my home during vacations?

- Do you think that any other job would accept such raunchy stupid-ass behavior?

- Do you have any medical conditions, such as OCD, ADHD, Tourette syndrome, psychosis, debilitating depression, multiple personalities, or any other physical or mental conditions that may interfere with the care given to your clients and in particular, me, so that I can make an informed decision as to whether I wish to have you in my home?

- Have you ever had a physical, and if so, what were the results?

- Do you often work quickly with no care about the efficiency of your work just so that you can get the hell out of there as fast as fucking possible?

- Are you a goddamn lazy person who just wants to collect a paycheck and has no pride in the work that his/her lazy ass has been assigned to do?

- Are you the type of person who will take advantage of a kind and sweet person, slowly and with intent getting more and more manipulative, thereby making your client uncomfortable and upset?

- Do you come into a client's home talking on your cell phone and keep on talking as long as you wish or talk whenever your phone rings, taking care of your personal business while you are at work?

- Do you really think that you would get away with that kind of inappropriate frickin' behavior in any other job?

- Are you short-tempered or do you get irritated with your client when she asks for things to be done in a particular way? Do you insist you have your own way of doing things, that you are in charge and no one is going to tell you any differently?

- Are you afraid of dogs, or do you have pet allergies?

41

A Suggested List of Questions to Ask Your Health Care Agency

When I first tried to find a Health Care Agency I had no idea where to start. The caseworker from the Department of Aging and Disability Services was not allowed to make recommendations and there was no rating system that I could find. I was given a long list of agencies and to my shock (not really) they all had such wonderful and caring names. Many had the word Angel, or Care or Blessing in their name so I just called several and hired the one that sounded the best. I hope that this questionnaire helps you to choose more easily and wisely than I did.

- How long has your agency been in existence?

- How many aides do you currently have?

- What kind of training do your aides receive?

- How long is the training period?

- What criteria do you have for hiring an aide?

- Do you always make sure that your client and the aide speak the same language?

- Do you sit down with your clients and explain to them that you want them to call the agency if they are uncomfortable with or intimidated by the aide?

- Do you do a background check on the aides?

- Are all of your aides here in the United States legally, either as citizens or through a work or student visa?

- Do you personally contact your client if an aide needs to go back to his/her country of origin for an extended period of time?

- Will you advise the client personally if the assigned aide will need to do this before you assign her to the client so that she can make an informed decision of whether this aide is an appropriate choice?

- It can be quite traumatic for your client to have to train and get used to another aide. That being said, do you make every effort to ensure that this will not happen?

- Has your agency or any of your aides been cited or reported to the state for any wrongdoings, and if so, what was the complaint?

- Do you regularly give random drug tests to your aides?

- Do you make sure that your aides have a yearly physical exam to confirm that they are physically able to do the job?

42

AND NOW FOR THE QUESTIONS I REALLY WOULD LIKE TO ASK MY HEALTH CARE AGENCY

Many of these questions come from my personal experience and will certainly be of interest to anyone who is seeking a health care agency.

- Are you in this business just for the money and to take advantage of Medicare and Medicaid programs and the clients in your care?

- How many aides do you currently have who are actually mentally and physically able to do the job?

- Do any of your aides actually receive any training whatsoever?

- If so, are your aides actually trained for more than a week?

- Do you have any criteria whatsoever for hiring your aides, or do you just take anyone off the street?

- Do you regularly put aides and clients together who do not speak the same goddamn language?

- Do you care at all if your clients are intimidated by, are uncomfortable with, or are scared shitless of the aides you have sent to them?

- Do at least 50 percent of your aides pass a background check?

- What percentage of your aides are actually here in the United States legally?

- If one of your aides needs to go back to his/her country of origin for any reason or needs to take off time from work do you leave it up to the clients to find out this shitty information on their own, putting them one step closer to wanting to harm you physically?

- Will you just have another shitty dumbass aide show up at the client's door if in fact his/her aide does need to leave for a period of time?

- Will you give your client the extra burden and stress of having to notify your sorry ass that his/her present aide is leaving for an extended period of time?

- Have you given any thought whatsoever to the trauma it can cause for your client to have to train and get used to another aide? If so, do you actually give a flying fuck?

- How many times have your aides or your agency been reported to the state for any wrongdoings, such as theft; manipulation; or physical, mental, sexual, or psychological abuse? You might as well tell me the truth now, because I'm going to find out one way or another.

- Do you ignore the evidence when you find out that your aides are doing illegal drugs, or do you actually encourage it?

- Does it make any difference at all to you if your aides are healthy enough, strong enough, and mentally sound enough to be taking care of elderly or disabled people, or are you just grateful to have any lame brained, hunchback, obese, sickly, criminal idiot show up to fill out an application so that you can collect even more money from the unsuspecting taxpayers?

43

POLICY FORM TO BE GIVEN TO ALL HOME HEALTH CARE AIDE APPLICANTS

You must go through an intensive training program and be able to complete certain tasks, which include:

- You must be able to lift and transfer the person in your care to and from the toilet, bed, shower, wheelchair, or anywhere else the patient wishes to go in a safe and strong manner, not putting him or her in any danger. Learn how to properly and safely help your patient to transfer and move about.

- You must always retain a professional manner, not discussing your personal problems, money problems, health issues, or your family information. You are there to care for your patient, not to burden him/her with problems of your own.

- You must not take or make personal calls while you are on the job. Handle your personal life when you are on your own time.

- You must pay attention to your patient and do things that he or she requests in a manner that you are told.

- You must never ask for food or drinks other than water while you are on your job.

- *Do not* take advantage of your patient's disability in any way, shape, or form. Your patient has you there because there are things that he/she can no longer do. He/she is in a vulnerable position, and taking advantage of him/her is unconscionable and will not be tolerated.

- Be on time. If you find it necessary to be late or cannot be there on the appointed day, make sure that you call your patient as soon as possible. Do not make the patient wait for you unnecessarily, thereby causing him/her stress and making him/her have to adjust his/her schedule to suit yours. And never make the patient have to track you down by calling you or the agency that has hired *you*.

- The person in your charge is your boss, and you will act accordingly by being polite, cheerful, and caring and by doing a professional and thorough job with whatever task is asked of you, just as you would with any other employer.

- Do not rush or cut corners so that you can get out of there as soon as possible. You are being paid with taxpayer money or money from the patient him/herself or his/her family, and therefore, you are expected to work hard and not to make excuses for a substandard work ethic.

- Laziness will not be tolerated. If you are asked to do something, do it with a concentrated effort and to the best of your ability. Take personal pride in your work, knowing that you are doing something of worth and importance. Not everyone is able to take on being a home health care aide, and if you do your job well, you are invaluable.

- Make sure that you ask your patient if there is anything else you can do for him/her before you leave. Make sure that he/she is comfortable and satisfied with the work you have done for him/her.

- If you have any questions about where something belongs or how the patient would like something to be done, ask him/her. Don't just put things where you feel like it or do things your own way no matter the consequences.

- Just because the person in your care has a disability does not mean that he/she is ignorant or not aware of your actions. Realize that it is hard for people with disabilities to ask for help and to be assertive, so it is up to you to make sure that things are done for their convenience and not for yours.

- Never put your patient in an uncomfortable position of having to be afraid of you or to feel that you will take measures to intimidate him/her by being verbally or physically abusive or by your body language. To do so is not only immoral but also illegal, and if you are such a person, you must be prepared to take the consequences.

- Do not ever ask your patient for money. It is cause for immediate dismissal.

- Do not complain about circumstances in your own life. The person in your care has enough to worry about and should not be put under any more stress than he/she already has.

- If you are tired or having a bad day, do not take it out on your patient. More than likely, he or she is having a much worse day than you are.

- Theft of any kind will not be tolerated; it is unconscionable, illegal, and cause for immediate dismissal as well as prosecution.

- If your patient is in a wheelchair or lying in bed, do not hover over him/her, thereby making the person uncomfortable because you are in a higher position. It is rude to your patient, and your job is to make him/her feel as good about him/herself as you possibly can.

- Always treat the person in your care as you would wish to be treated if you were in his/her situation. Be compassionate, caring, and helpful. There may come a day when you yourself will need the help of an aide. Act as the aide that you would wish to have in your home taking care of you.

44

And Now for the Policy Form I Really Would Like to Institute for All Home Health Care Aide Applicants

- If you are not able to lift and transfer your client in a strong and safe manner, you will spend four weeks in the army basic training program where you will learn the lesson of the necessity of being fit and strong.

- If you discuss any of your personal problems, such as money, health, or family situations, you will write a one-thousand-word essay on why you feel this is acceptable. It must be handwritten in a clear and precise form and be easily read. This is the lesson of setting and keeping the boundaries between yourself and the person you care for and not being a shithead.

- If you are using your cell phone while you are on the job to handle your own personal business, we will confiscate your phone and send it to our servicemen and women who are stationed overseas, so that you may learn the lesson of helping our heroes, who are on the job 24/7 with very little contact with their families. And just as a side note, I love you guys and gals, each and every one, and thank you for your service!

- If you insist on doing things your own way and not listening to how your patient wants things to be done, you will be sent to work cleaning up trash including drug paraphernalia and needles, used condoms, beer and liquor bottles, dog shit, and the occasional dead body in our public parks, including parks for children, for a period of three months, rain or shine, to include the months of July and August, so that you can learn the lesson of "just do your goddamn fucking job."

- If you ask the person in your care for anything other than water, you will clean out the entire refrigerator and eat the leftovers, including the ones that are covered in fucking mold or smell rancid. This lesson is to teach you how not to be a bloodsucking leech.

- If you are the type of unethical, slimy, ass wipe creep who would take advantage of someone's disability in any way, shape, or form, you will be sent to a women's prison for a period of sixty days where your roommate will be one big-ass lifer with tattoos all over her body, who will use you any way she sees fit. You gonna be her bitch! This is a lesson not to take advantage of those of us who need your help.

- If you are constantly late or don't show up on your appointed days without any notification, you must clean the patient's entire house, top to bottom, until it sparkles. That includes the filthy, dirty windows both fucking inside and fucking outside. This lesson is to teach you the art of respectful communication.

- If you do not respect the person in your care as your boss and are sassy or huffy or treat him or her gruffly or roughly, you will be made to go through a fraternity initiation, which you have to do in the buff (naked in front of the whole fraternity). This will teach you the lesson of who's the boss.

- If your workmanship is substandard and if you are lazy and just trying to scam money from the system, you will be audited by the IRS every year for the next fifteen years. And God help you if you're off by even one red cent. This will help teach you the virtue of honesty.

- If you really don't give a shit if your patient is comfortable and satisfied with your work, you will be taken to a laundromat and be put into a giant dryer and spun around on medium heat for a minimum of fifteen minutes and even more if you are especially lax. This will help you to learn the lesson of giving a shit.

- If you treat your clients like idiots, think you can get away with things just because they cannot get around, put things away wherever you feel like it, and just do things your own sloppy way knowing that many disabled people find it hard to be assertive, and feel that if you can get away with it, so much the better, then you will go to work in a homeless shelter doing laundry, preparing and serving meals, and helping to organize all of the various items needed to run the shelter. This will help you learn the lesson of humility.

- If you put your patient in a position of being afraid or intimidated in any way by your language, attitude, or by physical or verbal abuse, you will be sent to a South American prison for a period of no less than three years. This lesson is so you will know what it is like to be afraid and abused while being in a vulnerable position. American prisons, by comparison, are a dream vacation. I have seen that show *Imprisoned Abroad*, so I know a little about it; it looks god awful.

- If you hover over your client who is in a wheelchair or lying in bed and make him/her feel uncomfortable or threatened in any way or feel that you are in a higher position than he/she is, you will be put in the gorilla cage at the zoo so that you may learn the lesson of what it feels like to be at someone else's mercy.

- If you are treating the person in your care in a way that is uncompassionate, uncaring, unhelpful, and downright mean, then karma will someday, or perhaps some other lifetime, put you in the position that you put your client in, and you will learn the lesson of what it means to be abused by a caretaker, you fucking, demented, abhorrent piece of rhinoceros shit. And I mean that in a good way.

45

DATING A DISABILITY

Since I no longer have unfinished business with my ex-husband, Fuckwad (not his real name), there is a small voice in the back of my head that says, yes, when the time is right, I will have another man/companion/friend/lover come into my life. After several conversations with Dr. Cinzia about having another relationship, I have come to the conclusion that he would have to be a very spiritual person who was very special and was able to see the real me inside this weak, saggy-boobed, wheelchair-assed, left-side-paralyzed, potty-mouthed woman that I am.

And so my search begins. The first thing I did was to go online and search for websites that are specifically for disabled people. And what I found out is . . . *Oh, my God! What the fuck! Are you shitting me?* There are so many websites out there, and one of the most incredible and shocking things that I have learned is that there are able-bodied people who are looking specifically for disabled people to have relationships with. And get this; they are looking for specific disabilities! I kid you not. The list includes, in alphabetical order:

Acne scarring

ADD (attention deficit disorder)

Amputation

Anemia

Anxiety

Arm injury

Arthritis

Arthrogryposis

AS (Asperger's syndrome)

Asthma

Ataxia

Autism

Autoimmune disease

Back injury

Bipolar disorder

Blindness

Brain injury

Burn victim

Cancer

Cancer survivor

Cardiomyopathy

Cataract

Cerebral palsy

Leg disorder

Lung disease

Lupus

Lyme disease

Mastocytosis

ME (Myalgic encephalomyelitis)

Melanoma

Meniere's syndrome

MG (Myasthenia gravis)

Migraine

Moebius syndrome

Multiple sclerosis

Muscular dystrophy

Myopia

Narcolepsy

Neck injury

Neurological disorder

Obesity

Obsessive-compulsive disorder

Ostomy

Paralysis

Paraplegia

Parkinson's disease

Cerebral palsy

CFS (chronic fatigue syndrome)

Clubfoot

COPD (chronic obstructive pulmonary disease)

Corneal disease

Crohn's disease

Cystic fibrosis

Cystitis

Deafness

Dementia

Depression

Diabetes

Dialysis

Down syndrome

Dwarfism

Dyslexia

Dystonia

Ear disorders

Emphysema

Enuresis

Epilepsy

Fibromyalgia

Foot injury

Phobia

Polio

PPS (Postpolio syndrome)

PTSD (Post-traumatic stress disorder)

Pulmonary fibrosis

PWS (Prader-Willi syndrome)

Quadriplegia

Renal failure

RSD/(Reflex sympathetic dystrophy)

Schizophrenia

Scoliosis

Seizure

Sight impairment

Sjogren's syndrome

Sleep disorder

Speech impairment

Spina bifida

Spinal cord injury

Spondylitis

STD (Sexually transmitted disease)

Stroke survivor

Hemophilia

Head injury

Hearing impairment

Heart disorder

Hemiplegia

HIV

Huntington's disease

Hydrocephalus

Idiopathic hypersomnia

Incontinence

Kidney disease

Learning disability

TBI (Traumatic brain injury)

Tinnitus

TMAU

Tourette syndrome

Tuberculosis

Tumor, benign

Tumor, malignant

Vitiligo

Wheelchair-bound

I guess it really does go to prove that there is someone for everyone. And did you notice there are people who are looking for others with HIV and STDs? I think I will stick to men who are interested in women with MS and women in wheelchairs. That should give me enough material to work with. I'll just stick to what I know. About all the other stuff above, I do not know anything, nor do I want to.

I know there are a lot of sickos out there who prey upon the weakest in our society through manipulation and physical, psychological, sexual, and mental abuse. I myself have experienced several of these. And now, after going to therapy with Dr. Cinzia, who specializes in helping people with depression and serious illness, I have learned the signs of being taken advantage of and being abused psychologically and mentally. I am now able to make and keep clear boundaries in all of my relationships—particularly with the goddamn shitty aides that have come my way. Fuck them and the old nag they rode in on.

I have selected a new e-mail address and have four websites that look interesting and maybe promising. I will have to have Lara or Brian take a picture of me in all my stunning beauty so that I can upload it to the websites; they all say that I will not get responses unless there is a picture posted. So that is my next step.

Now mind you, for now, this is for research only; I am not going into this seriously looking for a man. I just think it is so interesting, and I really want to know, with my fucking inquiring mind who I may meet and learn about online, with a small possibility of meeting in person.

Dr. Cinzia and several of the websites I have visited have given stern advice to be very careful, because they could very well put me or other disabled men and women in danger if we don't do it properly and safely. There are predators out there specifically looking for disabled and vulnerable people strewn into the mix of men who are attracted to the self-assured and strong disabled women and, in particular, wheelchair-bound women who overcome obstacles.

Such men are attracted to the person who has the disability, not the disability itself. These men are called admirers. Devotees, on the other hand, are nondisabled people who are sexually attracted to people with disabilities; it is the disability that these people find appealing, not necessarily the person.

Pretenders are nondisabled people who act as if they have a disability by using assistive devices, such as wheelchairs or braces, and wannabes are people who actually want to become disabled, sometimes going to extraordinary lengths to have a limb amputated. I have found out that it is much more appealing to have a leg amputation above the knee than below the knee. I don't get it either, but who am I to judge?

I realize this is a lot to handle, so just take your time and digest the information.

So for now, I have a very interesting research project going on. I will write about it in detail, including the fellas I meet along the way, and will share those results in the sequel to this book at a later time. God willing. And who knows, maybe

I will find a companion along the way—a potty-mouth companion with a wicked sense of humor who would date me for me and not just my disability. Stranger things have happened.

46

CLOSE ENCOUNTER WITH
A GIANT

Christmas came and went quickly, as it always seems to do this time of year. The Mannheim Steamroller holiday concert was just wonderful, and a good time was had by all.

Sitting next to Lara in the gimp section at the concert was a young man who looked as though he was in his early 20's although it was hard to tell his age because he apparently has giantism which is defined by Webster's dictionary as: excessive growth of the body or any of its parts, especially as a result of over secretion of the growth hormone by the pituitary gland. It's also called *gigantism*. He was so tall, and his features and limbs were so misshapen that he had to travel in a wheelchair. He seemed so happy just to be out in the world; he was clearly enjoying being with a crowd and looking forward to a very exciting event, as was I.

Several of his family members, here on in to be known as the Grumpalumps, were there with him, and I was rather taken aback that not one of them seemed to talk or interact with him in any way, shape, or form. Lara spoke to him a little; he was hard to understand, but I did hear him say that it would be a night to be remembered. He had the largest feet and hands I had ever seen. His head was huge, and he had a very large, protruding forehead. His teeth were all askew. Nothing on his body seemed to match any of the other parts. He was fascinating to look at, but courtesy dictated that staring was not the thing to do. So I didn't.

After the concert, we happened to come across him again in the lobby. He was being pushed by one of the Grumpalumps in one direction, while Lara and I were going the opposite direction so that we met side by side. We stopped and agreed that the concert was truly a success, and as we were saying good-bye, I put out my hand to shake his. He took my hand, put it to his lips, and kissed it very sweetly and gently. I said, "Thank you," tearing up at the gentleness of this small act by this very large giant.

I heard Lara say, "Oooooooh!" She had also been touched by this moment in time. People were flowing this way and that all around us. Just then, for those thirty seconds, we really were being here now. If it were a scene in a movie, all the people in the background would be blurred and moving in slow motion, so that only the three of us would be privy to this small act of loveliness. His pusher decided he had had enough interaction for one evening and took him away, seemingly unaware of the magic of that moment and not in the least caring if he was ready to go or not.

We saw the giant one more time as we were sitting on the stone benches that are part of the inside architecture of the Myerson Theatre. We were waiting for the Handi-ride bus to pick us up and take Lara and I back home He was with three of the Grumpalumps; there was no smiling, no talking to each other, no joy amongst them. It was a sad, sad family, and my poor dear giant was at their mercy. They seemed to begrudge every step they took with and for him. This time, he didn't see us, and we watched as the Grumpalump dad parked their white van across the street and all of the Grumpalumps and the tender giant got in. I was surprised they didn't just forget about him and leave him stranded at the Myerson Theatre, either because they were unaware of his very existence or just so happy to finally be rid of him. They obviously had no idea how privileged they were to have him in their lives. I felt privileged to have been kissed by a truly gentle giant.

47

KOO KOO FOR COUPONS

My hobby with coupons and refunding, in the minds of Brian and Lara has become obsessive. Well, shit on a stick! They certainly don't mind when we always have shampoo, conditioner, deodorant, body wash, all sorts of over-the-counter medications and tons and tons of other stuff that end up costing nothing and in some cases can even make a profit. If my body were fully functioning I would be able to do so much more but because I have MS and am in a wheelchair I am just not able to do that anymore.

I only do a once a week trip to Walgreens and I have several favorite sites on the Internet where I get discounts or slightly damaged merchandise at great prices. It's all I can handle and the amount of work and organization that it takes to be able to do what I have learned to do is astronomical. So anyway I have just given it up to a higher power and just do what I can do on my own.

Oh! You're thinking to yourself, she's a hoarder. She's selfish and tries to get all the good stuff for herself. But that's where you would be wrong! My hobby not only provides all sorts of free products for my little family but I also give well over $10,000 a year worth of goods that I accumulate to homeless shelters and shelters for abused women and children. And I spend almost nothing on Christmas gifts because I take giant Christmas bags and fill them with a myriad of goodies that I have gotten for free or for very little and every one really looks forward to their goodie bags each year and seeing what surprises are inside.

My hobby gives me purpose, a reason to get out into the world, a way to contribute to our household and best of all to be able to give to people who are in dire straits and need a helping hand and I can do it generously on a Social Security disability income.

It keeps me from dwelling on what I can't do and focusing on what I can do which is a lot. It really is like having a full-time job because of the time, study, and organization that it takes to do this right. It keeps my mind active so I don't diminish into depression and loneliness and feeling sorry for myself. There are so many charities that are worthy and do so much good so I have chosen those that serve women and children and who provide a pickup service since I cannot bring the things to them. And I can't tell you the sense of satisfaction that I feel when the driver shows up and takes out the eight or 10 or 12 boxes and bags of wonderful stuff including clothing and toys and as many stuffed animals as I can accumulate.

And I just love the feeling of being able to make a difference, even if it's a small one that may bring some joy and comfort to someone who is lost or broken. I've been there and I know how it feels and it breaks my heart to see people go through much worse situations that I have ever gone through. So five or six times a year and in particular at Christmas time

I fill a bunch of boxes with stuff that I have accumulated in my walk-in closet and give it away.

I've heard it said many times from many experts that the best way to help yourself whether you suffer from depression or illness or are just down in the dumps is to do something good for someone else and I can attest to you that it is true; it really does work. So look, if I can do the little that I am able to do being paralyzed on the left side of my body, in a wheelchair with MS and am fatigued much of the time, think about what you could do to make the world a better place and not dwell on what is negative but rather on how much better the world would be if we all just give a little bit, do a little bit, help a little bit.

So my suggestion to anyone is to get off your sorry ass and do something good even if it means having a better attitude and not blaming everyone else for your problems and putting on a smile and helping the little old lady cross the street or visiting your grandmother in a nursing home. That's a good start. Build from there and do yourself proud.

And I am not saying this to sing my own praises because I've come a long way in the course of my therapy to realize that I am still powerful in spite of disability. Not powerful in ways that I used to be but in ways that I have adapted to and a mindset that has taken a 180 degree turn from being depressed to the point of thinking of suicide to a point where I am actually writing a book and doing what writers are supposed to do which is to write about what they know.

And what I know is we are here on earth to learn. And as Maya Angelo states so eloquently, "We do the best we know how and when we know better we do better." And I believe that that means to forgive yourself for past mistakes. It means to not dwell upon them but learn from them and go on to do bigger and better things and thereby go on to be a bigger and better person.

Okay enough of my blah, blah, blah do-gooder lecture. Just a little fuckin food for fuckin thought. Just because I do what I can for charitable organizations doesn't mean that I still don't have a potty mouth. Nuff said.

48

AND THE WINNER IS

Ladies and Gentleman, the moment you've all been waiting for: let's give a big rousing round of applause for the list of nominees in the category of person having the most influence in the writing of this book.

And the nominees are:

Bryan Grayson photography . . . for taking the cover images and turning a bald man into a fully haired woman. Without him the cover would not be the same and it wouldn't make any sense. He also did my cover photo and I don't look like a bald man. I am grateful.

Dr. Ruth . . . for her wonderful work in teaching women how to pleasure themselves;

Kenny Rogers . . . for helping me to learn the lesson of when to fold 'em;

Shady Ray . . . for being my brother after all these years;

Dr. Cinzia . . . because without her, I never would have become unstuck and this book would never have been written;

Dr. Ick . . . for helping me to recognize the series of men who have taken advantage of my naïveté and vulnerability;

Schmuck . . . for being there in a place and time when I was strong enough to say, "Stop it with the schemes and just do your frickin' job";

Dolly Parton . . . for bringing such joy to my mom throughout the years, so much so that during her grand mal seizure, she took on your persona—that is the ultimate tribute she could give to you . . . making her your number-one fan;

Smashing Pumpkins . . . for being so good to my son, little six-year-old Ryan;

Tiny Tim . . . just for being your freaky little self;

Transvestite Murderer . . . for hiring me and giving me the experience of working for a real, live murderer;

Blind Divorce Lawyer . . . for being tough for me when I couldn't be tough for myself.

Elvis Costello . . . for giving Lara and me the great pleasure of seeing your show;

Fuckwad . . . for giving me such great material from which to grow and blossom—in good times and in bad, you will always be Fuckwad to me;

The Nazi Family . . . for giving me so much food for thought and the chance to push myself at a time when I had so little confidence—I did many things I never thought possible;

Cheapwad . . . for helping me to realize myself worth was more than your eyes beheld

Bad Cabbie . . . for making me realize the power of my intuition—that little voice in my head that says, "This is not right . . . Beware":

Benjamin Franklin . . . for inventing the catheter, for bringing into reality the library system, and of course, for being one of the founding fathers of the United States of America;

Oprah! . . . for bringing the world to a much higher spiritual realization and for making such a huge difference in my personal life as well—No more need be said. She's Oprah for God's sake!

Lipstick Fetish Guy . . . for being my first friend when I came to Texas, when I was scared and alone, and for taking me under his wing. He helped me to get my feet on the ground and prove that I have an A-OK pussy;

Sleep Pisser . . . for making my hospital stay even more exciting;

Big Black Haitian Aide . . . for helping me to see the pattern of men who found in me an easy, vulnerable target to take advantage of;

Kool and the Gang . . . for giving Lara and me a reason to celebrate;

Various Handi-ride Bus Drivers . . . thank you one and all—I appreciate the bus service so much; the amount of independence it gives those of us with mobility problems is invaluable;

OCD Aide (Not Her Real Name) . . . for giving me yet another opportunity to buck up and learn to be assertive;

Gentle Giant . . . for touching my heart at the symphony.

Scary Amazon Woman Aide . . . for starting me on my path of learning how to set boundaries and not let things get out of hand;

Mafioso Murderer . . . for being such an idiot and finally being in prison where you belong, you wicked, wicked man;

Nurse Who Shared the Royal Wedding with Me . . . for giving me the opportunity to turn the tables and make a friend and advocate out of a bad first impression.

Hand me the envelope please . . .

Oh my God!

We have two second-place winners! It's a tie between . . . *Dolly Parton* and *Benjamin Franklin*! Congratulations to both of you!

And that means the winner is . . .

Fuckwad!

For all of the material that you have added to the book;

For all of the opportunities for self-growth;

For all of the incidences to be seen as chances for healing the past and reclaiming my now;

And so, Fuckwad, I forgive you, I wish you well, I wish you prosperity and health in mind, body, and spirit, and last but not least, God bless you.

49

Stuck to Nevermore Stuck

The poem that follows, "Nevermore Stuck," depicts how I feel after almost two years of therapy and shedding the fear and grief and shame little by little along the way. The therapy sessions took me in directions that I never would have imagined could have such a huge impact on how I shaped and lived my life. I have gone from a place of being totally lost and stuck to a place where I have actually written a published book in which I relive and share my insights for the whole world to see. It's been a long and painful road. I am not there yet, but I know I am on the right path, so I will just keep stumbling along, or rolling along in my wheelchair, as the case may be.

And for the first time in so many years, I am so very proud.

Nevermore Stuck

Where once I was stuck

in this chair with wheels and in legs that don't work,

and in this body that won't move when I tell it to,

yell it to, scream it to, cry, and weep and beg it to.

Circuitry still gone awry.

And yet I am stuck no more.

I found a way out, a way in, a way around

and between and through.

I now know what to do;

I have succumbed, retreated, relented;

I have seeped inside myself, my mind, my soul

I have found peace, acceptance, dignity, joy,

spiritual self, a reason to live, love, hope, courage,

faith, miracles, something that has relieved the

ache so that I will be

Nevermore Stuck

THE END

CPSIA information can be obtained at www.ICGtesting.com
Printed in the USA
LVOW08s1103081113

360549LV00001B/5/P